The Gospels and Rabbinic Judaism

The Gospels and Rabbinic Judaism

A Study Guide

Michael Hilton
with
Gordian Marshall OP

KTAV PUBLISHING HOUSE, INC.
HOBOKEN, NEW JERSEY

ANTI-DEFAMATION LEAGUE B'NAI B'RITH
NEW YORK, NEW YORK

Library of Congress Cataloging-in-Publication Data

Hilton, Michael.
  The Gospels and Rabbinic Judaism.

  Bibliography: p.
  Includes indexes.
  1. Bible. N.T. Gospels—Comparative studies.
2. Rabbinical literature—Relation to the New Testament.
I. Marshall, Gordon. II. Title.
BS2555.5.H54 1988   226'.06   88-18260
ISBN 0-88125-303-0

        Manufactured in the United States of America

    First published by SCM PRESS LTD. London, England

Contents

To the Sisters at Ammerdown Study Centre
in recognition of the work they and the
Sisters of Sion have done for Jewish-Christian
understanding

Preface

This work brings together texts from early rabbinic writings and the Gospels. The aim is to make primary sources available to adults and young people who are interested in inter-faith issues but who may have no prior knowledge of this field. The choice of texts is not intended to be exhaustive: we have chosen to give examples which illustrate different types of comparison which can be made, touching on topics of relevance to Jewish-Christian dialogue today.

The texts presented also reflect the huge variety of types of rabbinic literature. It is not within the scope of this work to review what rabbinic literature is, and what it contains. Some brief guidance will be found in the glossary of Hebrew terms at the end of this work. The reader who requires more detailed information is referred to one of the many books available: one which is most useful for rabbinic literature is R. C. Musaph-Andriesse's book *From Torah to Kabbalah: A Basic Introduction to the Writings of Judaism*. This work has been translated from the Dutch by John Bowden, and is easily obtainable. This and the other works referred to are listed in the Bibliography.

The methodology of this work is experimental in the sense that the research done has been to present the texts and note reactions from Jews and Christians: many such reactions have been used in the discussion of the texts here. The material was presented in its entirety in a week's study course, taught jointly by Michael Hilton and Gordian Marshall, at the Ammerdown Conference Centre near Bath in August 1986. Some of the material has also been taught in March and April 1987 in the Cornerstone Programme at Westminster Cathedral, and to various other groups. Published secondary material has been referred to only when essential.

Although the principal aim is to let the texts speak for themselves, inevitably the opinions and approach to the texts of the authors are very important. The most obvious area in which this is important is the question of translation, since the texts are not here offered in the original languages, but in English versions. When translating from one language to another, there is some-times no exact equivalent for a word or phrase, and a sentence has to be dismantled and reassembled in a different way. This is a particularly acute problem with the Hebrew texts, for the simple reason that Hebrew, being a semitic language, is much further removed from English than the Greek of the Gospels: it is much easier to find English equivalents for Greek words than for Hebrew. The reader should also be aware of the difficulties of transferring terms from one religion to another: for example, both traditions use words such as 'sin', 'repentance' and 'forgiveness' but what is meant by them is often very different. The translations of Hebrew texts are our own: for the Gospels the Revised Standard Version has been followed throughout. The system of transliteration of Greek and Hebrew words follows the General System used by *Encyclopedia Judaica*, except that *tz* is used here for the letter *tzadi*. All transliterated words are given in *italics*, except for four which occur very frequently: Mishnah, Talmud, Torah and Shabbat.

Ideally, the units should be studied by Jews and Christians together, either in pairs or in small groups. It is recommended that the introduction to each unit is read as far as the first study text. Then the study texts for the unit can be studied and discussed, initially without the aid of any commentary. It will readily be found that Jews and Christians have very different ways of looking at the texts, and different attitudes and preconceptions. Questions which will be found useful for discussion include 'What is this text about?' 'What point was its author or compiler trying to make?' 'What does it mean to Jews today?' 'What does it mean to Christians today?'

The commentaries provided here will provide some guide to answering these questions. Inevitably, a lively discussion will raise many other and different issues. In commenting on the texts, we have felt free to follow chains of thought which lead from one text or topic to another, rather than dealing fully and systematically with every detail. This kind of free ranging discussion is typical of much rabbinic writing.

The book can also be used as a reference book, or used by study groups of one faith, or by those reading alone. But that is not its principal purpose: this work is one which aims to bring together Jews and Christians in a common study enterprise. That is why the reader will find included here not just the normal material of academic study, but issues which are important in the dialogue world of our own time.

Preface to the American Edition

In our time Christians and Jews have reached a unique moment in their history. Together, talking to each other, they are sharing a hope for the future rooted in a new time of discovery and interdependence.

It has not been an easy process. We have been and still are, in some respects, in confrontation. Ironically, the interpretation of the Scriptural texts on which we base our faith traditions has been a battleground for centuries. This struggle over the "correct" interpretation of the Hebrew Bible and the New Testament has entailed victories and defeats, arrogance of power and persecution. It also has been largely indifferent to the human situation of Christians and Jews, and its consequences have been to relegate the Jewish people to an alienated existence and second-class citizenship.

We begin this new time in our history aware of the ever-present danger of antisemitism, which took its most diabolic shape during the Second World War when six million Jews perished under Nazi totalitarianism. Despite and because of this evil and horror, Christians and Jews are now coming together in a process of recognition and understanding.

The distinguishing mark of this new relationship is the knowledge of the other as a person of God. It is essentially a relationship of mutual esteem. Both partners of the encounter are peers before God, companions in an eternal design of redemption. Christians and Jews in dialogue are equals in front of God, equals in front of each other.

The recognition of our separate but spiritually related identities is enhanced by a respectful acceptance of each other, and a mutual knowledge of our faith commitments. This mutual knowledge increases awareness of our own traditions and spiritualities: the living experience of our commitment in the daily life of individuals and the community. It is done in order to be enlightened by the other person's faith. It is not syncretism, the mixture of traditions, but the knowledge of differences as a source for deepening our responses to God and each other.

To study their own tradition and the tradition of the other is a necessity and a duty for those engaged in dialogue. The editors of this book, Rabbi Michael Hilton and Father Gordian Marshall, attempt to bring together Christians and Jews in the study of sources and how we today can respond in their light to problems affecting both communities. It is done in a spirit of shared community, a spirit which is central in Judaism and Christianity alike.

The Gospels and Rabbinic Judaism emphasizes the study of our foundational texts. It is important for both Christians and Jews to understand the root, the Hebrew Bible (*Tanakh*), and the branches that sprang from it, the rabbinic and early Christian interpretations. Christians and Jews need to study each other's sources as well as their own, to become familiar with aspects of our separate spiritualities and the common ground between them.

The Christian exploration of rabbinic sources is an excursion into Jesus' spiritual formation. Without its knowledge, a Christian is uprooted from the basic reality of his/her commitment. The U.S. Catholic bishops thus state:

> Most essential concepts in the Christian creed grew at first in Judaic soil. Uprooted from that soil, these basic concepts cannot be perfectly understood. It is for reasons such as these that the Second Vatican Council in *Nostra Aetate* recommends joint "theological and biblical studies" with Jewish scholars. The renewal of Christian faith is the issue here, for renewal always entails to some extent a return to one's origin. (National Conference of Catholic Bishops, November, 1975.)

Similarly, a recent Presbyterian statement explains:

> Christianity began in the context of Jewish life and faith. Jesus was a Jew as were his earliest followers . . . The life and liturgy of the Jews provided the language and thought forms through which the revelation in Jesus was first received and expressed.

And the 1987 United Church of Christ statement concludes that "the New Testament can only be adequately understood in the light of (the) common heritage with the Jewish people."

For the Jew, a study of the Gospels is one way to recover a sense of the society and spiritual trends of the early rabbinic currents. Dr. David Flusser, professor of early Christianity at the Hebrew University in Jerusalem, has explained this need to know Christian writings in his recent volume, *Jewish Sources in Early Christianity (I)*:

Jewish sources alone cannot teach us enough about Second Temple Judaism. Our information on rabbinic Judaism from these sources, for example, dates from a few generations after the rise of Christianity. The Sages began to chronicle their own history only after the destruction of the Second Temple (70 C.E.) and most of those who recorded their earlier tradition in the Midrashim (Books of Biblical Exegesis) and in the rabbinic legends lived at least a generation after the destruction of the Temple or later. Nevertheless, even the superficial reader of these sources will soon find that they reflect an old tradition which in many cases is considerably earlier than the period of those in whose names it is reported.

The study of the sources is an invitation to friendship. It is a way to deepen our comprehension of our respective traditions as partners in God's Covenant. To study together is to build bridges of peace. We are inviting you to do so by using *The Gospels and Rabbinic Judaism* in your congregation's adult education program or as the text for a Christian and Jewish study group. The first century rabbi, Simeon ben Lakish, said: "God loves two students who arrange to study *halachah* together." (Talmud Shabbat 63A). And Mishnah *Aboth* comments: "When two sit together and words of Torah pass between them, then God's presence rests on them" (3:3).

Dr. Eugene J. Fisher, National Conference of Catholic Bishops, Secretariat for Catholic-Jewish Relations.

Rabbi Leon Klenicki, Anti-Defamation League of B'nai B'rith, Department of Interfaith Affairs.

Rev. Jay Rock, National Council of Churches, Office of Jewish-Christian Relations.

Introduction

It is often stated that Jews worship with their heads covered because Christians pray bareheaded. Whether that is the real origin of Jewish headcoverings is lost in the mists of medieval history: what is important is that people believe this to be the origin, and still feel it to be a distinction worth keeping. It is thus a commonplace idea that Judaism and Christianity have developed many practices in contradistinction to each other, practices born out of centuries of enmity and misunderstanding.

Today, the hatred of the past has been replaced by rivalry. It is all too easy for those involved in Jewish-Christian dialogue to adopt a competitive spirit, of holding discussions in which their motive is simply to prove their own faith superior to the other. Such debates do nothing to help us realize how an understanding of the other tradition can help enhance our understanding of our own faith. This work has been written on the assumption that the reader is interested in learning about both traditions, and how they can illuminate each other. Inevitably each of us is bound to feel that some texts are more relevant to our own lives than others: that we feel more at home with our own tradition. But that does not mean that other texts are of no value, and have nothing to teach us.

A brief example will show how a comparative study can be helpful. The process of contradistinction between the two faiths is as old as those faiths. One early rabbinic work is known as *Pirke Avot* – Sayings of the Fathers. The 'Fathers' were the early rabbis and the scholars whose traditions they inherited. Jesus in the Gospels is called 'Rabbi'. (The word 'Rabbi' is Hebrew for 'my master'.) Today, Jewish scholars are still called by the title 'Rabbi', and many Christian priests by the name 'Father'. Yet nobody would dream of calling a Christian leader 'Rabbi' or a Jewish leader 'Father'. The adoption of the title by one group has precluded its use by the other. The two titles started as a common heritage, but became divided.

When did the divisions begin? An examination of the use of the title 'Rabbi' in Jewish and Christian texts can help to clarify this.

At the beginning of Chapter 23 of Matthew's Gospel there is a passage of bitter criticism of the behaviour of the Pharisees (Matt. 23.1–10):

> Then said Jesus to the crowds and to his disciples, 'The scribes and the Pharisees sit on Moses' seat; so practise and observe whatever they tell you, but not what they do; for they preach, but they do not practise. They bind heavy burdens, hard to bear, and lay them on men's shoulders; but they themselves will not move them with their finger. They do all their deeds to be seen by men; for they make their phylacteries broad and their fringes long, and they love the place of honour at feasts and the best seats in the synagogues, and salutations in the market places, and being called rabbi by men. But you are not to be called rabbi, for you have one teacher, and you are all brethren. And call no man your father on earth, for you have one Father, who is in heaven. Neither be called masters, for you have one master, the Christ.'

In John there are texts where Jesus is himself called Rabbi: John 1.38; 1.49; 3.2; 6.25. The first example is from a narrative in which Jesus is collecting his disciples around him:

> Jesus turned, and saw them following, and said to them, 'What do you seek?' And they said to him, 'Rabbi' (which means Teacher), 'where are you staying?' (1.38)

John the Baptist is also called 'Rabbi' in John's Gospel (3.26).

In the text from Matthew, Jesus objects to the use of titles for religious leaders: already he seems to be making a distinction between his followers and the Jewish teachers who 'love . . . being called rabbis by men'. The text seems to suggest that 'Rabbi' was a popular title at the time of Jesus. Was this really so?

A great deal of evidence about the titles actually used by Jewish scholars at the time is collected in 'Sayings of the Fathers'. This little book is part of the Mishnah, a Jewish text compiled about 200 CE, but containing much older material (the meaning of the terms 'Mishnah' and 'CE', and other terms used here, will be found in the Glossary at the end of this work). 'Sayings of the Fathers' describes how Jewish teachings were handed down from generation to generation, and gives names of teachers who lived in each generation. It begins:

> Moses received Torah on Sinai, and handed it down to Joshua;
> Joshua to the elders; the elders to the prophets; and the prophets
> handed it down to the Men of the Great Assembly. . . . Simon
> the Just was one of the last survivors of the Great Assembly.

Simon the Just is thought to have lived in the second century BCE.
The text goes on to describe how he handed knowledge of the
tradition to a man called Antignos of Sokho, and he to other
teachers. Various names follow, all without title attached.

Eventually we read how the tradition passed to two teachers
called Shemaiah and Avtalion, who lived in the first century BCE,
and Hillel and Shammai, who were older contemporaries of Jesus
himself. None of them is ever referred to as Rabbi: another text
calls Hillel and Shammai the 'fathers of the world' (Mishnah
Eduyot 1.4). After giving many of the teachings of Hillel and
Shammai, 'Sayings of the Fathers' (the Hebrew title is *Pirke Avot*)
goes on to a man called *Rabban* Gamaliel – he is mentioned in Acts
(5.34; 22.3). This title *Rabban* is also used of Yohanan ben Zakkai.
He was the Jewish teacher who survived the destruction of
Jerusalem and the Temple in the year 70 CE, and according to
legend settled and founded a new academy in a place called Yavneh
(Jamnia), thus ensuring the survival of the Jewish tradition. This
word *Rabban* seems to have been the Aramaic equivalent of *Nasi*
('chief'), and indicates that Gamaliel and Yohanan were head of the
rabbinical courts of their day. It seems that this post was
distinguished by a special title. As the tradition continued to be
passed on from one generation to the next, Yohanan ben Zakkai
had five main disciples, and *Pirke Avot* gives them the title 'Rabbi'
(*Avot* 2.10): Rabbi Eliezer ben Hurkanos, Rabbi Joshua ben
Hananya, Rabbi Yossi HaCohen, Rabbi Shimon ben Natanel, and
Rabbi Elazar ben Arakh. All of them grew up after the year 70.
There are many other rabbinic texts which mention the names
listed in 'Sayings of the Fathers' and these texts show a remarkable
consistency of the use of titles: Hillel and Shammai are never
called Rabbi, and Yohanan ben Zakkai only *Rabban*.

So it seems that the title Rabbi was first used of the disciples of
Rabban Yohanan ben Zakkai. According to Jewish tradition, he
lived to be a hundred and twenty years old. This should not be
regarded as an exact figure, but one often used for a full life, because
Moses according to Deuteronomy lived to be a hundred and twenty
years old. Yohanan lived for about ten years after the destruction of
Jerusalem in 70, but no doubt was very old at the time: although he

is chiefly known for his teachings in Yavneh at the end of his life, he could well have had disciples earlier than that before the destruction. One of these disciples was in fact called by the title *Rabbi*. This was a man called Hanina ben Dosa. Now he was a very interesting figure, in that unlike the later rabbis, he does not appear to have been a scholar, but a miracle worker. There is a very good discussion of the legends about him in Geza Vermes, *Jesus the Jew*. This is an unusual book, in that it does not deal with Jesus' life and teachings in any kind of narrative way, but rather with the titles used about Jesus: Jesus the prophet, Jesus the Lord, Jesus the Messiah. Strangely, he says very little about Jesus the Rabbi, which he mentions only in passing. But he does retell many of the strange legends about Hanina ben Dosa, and the reader is referred to this book for further information about him. It is noteworthy that he was called Rabbi, and like Jesus, lived earlier than others called by that title: and like him was famous as a miracle worker. Was the title Rabbi in any way connected with miracle workers?

There is a relevant text at the end of Tosefta *Eduyot*, to be dated from its contents about the third generation after the destruction of 70:

> He who has disciples, and his disciples again have disciples, is called Rabbi: when his disciples are forgotten he is called Rabban: and when the disciples of his disciples are also forgotten he is called simply by his name.

The author is saying that he calls his grandfather's generation *Rabbi*: the generation before that *Rabban*: and any generation before that simply by their names.

This small point about the use of the title 'Rabbi' thus raises a great many difficulties. How could the scholars of Jesus' day love to be called 'Rabbi' if the word was not used as a title at that time? When was Jesus himself first called 'Rabbi'?

Our analysis suggests that Matthew's text may well not reflect an actual sermon given by Jesus, but the situation at the time Matthew's Gospel was written, when enmity between the early Christian and the Jewish communities was already hardening. It seems unlikely that the title 'Rabbi' was in common usage before 70 CE, and the debate probably took place after that date. We cannot assume that because Matthew says Jesus was critical of the Pharisees calling themselves Rabbi, that this is exactly what happened. The title seems to have developed in the half century after Jesus, and was therefore an issue not in Jesus' time, but later, at the time when the Gospel was written. We have to understand the Gospel tradition in its own terms, always remembering that such debates reflect the period before and after the destruction of Jerusalem when all the different groupings were rethinking their functions, theologies, titles and so on. The changes around that time were immense and significant.

Note how Jesus also objected to the use of the term 'Father'. The objection to the term 'Rabbi' persisted, as this was the title which became common for Jewish teachers, but Christian priests later came to be called 'Father'. Some have even sought to deny that Jewish teachers were ever called Father: they suggest that the title *Pirke Avot* does not really mean 'Sayings of the Fathers', but refers to another use of the word *Avot* in the sense of 'important subjects or categories'. (This use of the word will be discussed further in Units Four and Five below, pp. 83 and 98.) How could Jews have used a Christian term! In fact the term *Avot* may deliberately have been chosen for this work in order to include the early teachers, before the title 'Rabbi' was used.

The example of the use of the term 'Rabbi' has been treated at some length, because it encapsulates many of the difficulties of a comparative study.[1] When looked at side by side, the Jewish and Christian texts often appear to mean something very different from the way they normally appear. Anybody who compares such texts for the first time will encounter a great deal of shock and surprise. Christian readers may be surprised to discover that texts such as Matthew's 'love to be called rabbi by men' cannot be substantiated by rabbinic texts for Jesus' day: Jewish readers new to the Gospels are likely to be shocked by the portrayals of the Pharisees found there. For that reason, this work does not present the texts simply in an academic fashion, but attempts to spell out many of the reactions Jews and Christians may have to them. Only if we are open about our shock and surprise can dialogue proceed.

There is a vast amount of secondary material on Jesus and his Jewish background, or Jewish views of Jesus. Over two hundred books in this field are estimated to have been published over the past one hundred years. This work adopts a 'back to the sources' approach and bases itself principally on primary sources – the words of the ancient evangelists and rabbis themselves. Although there are great differences between rabbinic and Christian literature of the first two centuries CE, the comparisons here are much more a comparison of like with like than the more usual process of reading the Gospels in the light of the teaching of the Hebrew Bible. To understand the Gospels, it is surely necessary to understand not only the biblical background, but something about Jewish teaching at the time the Gospels were written. Sometimes, too, the Gospels can shed fresh light on rabbinic texts.

The aim of this work, then, is to provide a course or reference book containing primary sources on the subject and guidelines for their study by those who are interested in inter-faith issues but who may have no prior knowledge of this field. The discussions of the material inevitably do not illuminate or elucidate every aspect of the texts, although care has been taken to write about those aspects of the texts which have particular relevance to Jewish-Christian dialogue today.

The main topics covered are 'the great commandment', the synagogue and its function, the parable, the Sabbath, divorce, and forgiveness. In addition there is included an introduction to rabbinic legal studies under the title 'The Ox in the Pit' (Unit Four). These topics differ not only in subject matter, but also in the type of comparison offered – legal, historical, literary, theological or even contrasting themes. Inevitably, other important topics have been left out, such as 'resurrection', 'salvation', 'Messiah'. The topic of attitudes to miracles is not treated separately, although 'healing' receives some discussion in Units Five and Seven.

The problem of dating texts would at first sight appear to make it very difficult to compare the rabbinic and Gospel texts. Most of the rabbinic texts available for comparison were compiled at the end of the second century CE, while Jesus lived at the beginning of the first century CE. However, the real gap in dating is not as great as it at first appears. The oral transmission of rabbinic ideas was very important, and the rabbinic texts clearly reflect much earlier material. It will be seen how many rabbinic debates reflect the new situation which existed after the destruction of Jerusalem and the temple in the year 70, when Judaism had to adapt to a totally new situation. Many of the Gospels, too, reflect controversies of exactly this same period, which was also a period of crisis for the early Christian communities. The criticism here offered of the Gospels is of the type known as 'redaction criticism': that is to say, it tries to interpret the texts as they were written: no real attempt is made here to get behind the texts to the 'historical Jesus'. There are many excellent works on that field: this work makes no attempt to be one of them.

For the reasons stated above in the discussion of the title 'Rabbi', it seems likely that much of the lively controversy in the Gospels supports the theory that they were all written after 70. Further evidence to support the line adopted here will be found in the course of studying the texts.

This work follows the consensus of scholarly opinion that Mark's is the earliest Gospel, then Matthew, then Luke, and then John. Matthew and Luke clearly made great use of Mark, and these three are known as the Synoptic Gospels. They were all probably written by the early 80s CE. John's Gospel is rather later, and reflects a time when attitudes between the various communities had hardened still further, both between Jew and Christian, and between the various Christian communities:[2] John requires a rather different kind of approach from the Synoptic Gospels, and is therefore little used for the purposes of this study. Matthew is generally thought to have had the best knowledge of rabbinic Judaism, and for that reason his version has generally been selected here, although it will be seen that Luke and John also had a great deal of independent knowledge of aspects of Jewish life and thought.

Ideally, the units should be studied by Jews and Christian together, either in pairs or small groups, but the work will be found to be equally useful for reference, or for those studying alone.

There are different kinds of dialogue. There is the kind where people of different faiths meet and talk face to face and try to learn from each other, and there is the kind where they look at texts and history, and try to learn from that. Each of these two has its difficulties. The difficulty of just talking is that there soon comes a point where one wishes to be anchored in a tradition, to know the origins of theologies and prejudices. It can be an aimless and a restless enterprise to talk without knowing the texts and the history from which our ideas spring. The problem with the other kind of dialogue – the kind based on texts – is that sometimes we can use those texts as an escape, to avoid looking at ourselves and our feelings. We cannot confront texts unless we first confront ourselves.

Every reader who approaches the texts with an open mind will learn something new about *both* traditions, for the texts will be found to illuminate each other, and give a clear understanding both of the similarities and differences between the two faiths. From reading the texts side by side it will become clear how and why Jewish and Christian viewpoints on many issues have developed in contradistinction to each other, while in other fields the viewpoints show a remarkable similarity – one greater than many realize.

From any reading of these texts, questions for dialogue will emerge – questions which spring from the texts but are not in themselves part of them – questions relevant to our own lives. Some suggested questions for discussion are included here – it is not suggested that they are the only ones which might emerge or even the most important: the points for discussion do, however, reflect questions students have actually asked themselves and each other on studying the texts.

Dialogue is easiest for those anchored securely in their own tradition: it is more difficult for those who have many doubts as to which faith they should belong to, or for those who see themselves equally part of both traditions. This is because it is a mistake to imagine that we can equate one element in Christianity with a similar element in Judaism, or *vice versa*. Each faith says something which makes sense, but if we mix them up, we shall find only confusion. Just as it is impossible to merge two different languages and speak in a mixture of both, so the texts here do not have a central point of meeting or equation, although at times they parallel each other in their own languages. Sometimes the same question or theme will emerge, but it is handled differently because of different interests or expectations. At other times, where one might expect the same question to arise, it does not: the same text or theme might lead to completely different reactions and questions. Those who find that the material here leads to severe religious doubts about previously accepted traditions are strongly advised to consult a rabbi or priest from their own tradition. This is a new enterprise, and it is bound to provoke strong or unexpected reactions from some. It is important not to be alone at such a time.

The Great Commandment

Initial point of comparison:
Theological

The aims of this unit are:

1. To demonstrate by means of an example how the Gospels and the rabbis shared various ethical concerns.

2. To introduce the necessary skills required for reading the texts.

3. To show some of the difficulties of deciding 'Who said it first?' and 'Who said it best?'

The subject matter of this unit is 'the great commandment'. Is there a commandment which sums up how I must behave before God? The idea of a simple, snap formula is clearly appealing. We shall read first rabbinic texts, and after that Gospel texts which deal with this question in a similar way. The standard modern treatment of this subject was written sixty years ago – Chapter 2 of Israel Abrahams, *Studies in Pharisaism and the Gospels*, First Series, Cambridge University Press 1917. In spite of its age, this sets out the facts more clearly than any more recent work.

In Matthew 22.34–40 Jesus refers to 'You shall love the Lord with all your heart and with all your soul, and with all your might' (Deut. 6.5) as 'the great and first commandment' and 'You shall love your neighbour as yourself' (Lev. 19.18), as 'a second commandment'. This provides an initial point of comparison to several rabbinic texts.

The rabbinic texts given here quote from the period from Hillel to Rabbi Akiva, whose lives span about a hundred and fifty years from the beginning of the first to the middle of the second century CE.

Skills

Some basic skills are required in order to read any rabbinic or Gospel texts with insight and understanding.

Rabbinic Texts

It is difficult, but not impossible, to approach rabbinic texts without a knowledge of Hebrew. Any translation is at best an approximation. In translating rabbinic texts, where often the idioms are very far from those naturally used in English, a literal translation can be very difficult to follow, while a free translation, which adds something by way of explanation, often selects only one of a number of possible meanings. In translating the texts in this work we have tried to steer midway between these two extremes.

The reader of this Unit will come across a number of the difficulties involved in reading such texts. The most obvious difficulty is the use of biblical quotation in a way which often seems far from the simple meaning of the text. Such use of quotation is known as *midrash*, from a root which means 'to seek' or 'to enquire into'. Because not everything we need to know is stated explicitly in the scriptures, *midrash* seeks to delve deeper than the surface meaning, to draw out interpretations which are not immediately obvious.

The reader will find it helpful to look up all biblical quotations mentioned in the rabbinic texts. This is because the context of the quotation is sometimes very important, and the words quoted may be only part of the quotation needed. However, the rabbis were not averse to lifting phrases completely out of context, and examples of this can also readily be found. There is no simple way of knowing when the context is going to be important and when not: so every text should be looked up and the context examined.

One principle of rabbinic interpretation which is very important is the idea that there is no redundant word in Torah: any phrase which seems to be a mere repetition in fact carries within it a distinct and precise significance. This principle derives from the belief that the Torah is the word of God, and so its words must be endowed with a depth of meaning which is greater than mere human utterance. For example, in the first line of the *Shema*, 'Hear, O Israel, the Lord is our God, the Lord is One' (Deut. 6.4), the Rabbis wanted to know why the word 'Lord' is repeated, when the text could simply have said 'The Lord our God is one'. Some of the answers will be studied in this unit.

Sometimes rabbinic interpretation seems to limit or restrict the plain meaning of a text, sometimes to expand it. In this unit we shall be discussing various interpretations of Leviticus 19.18, 'You shall love your neighbour as yourself: I am the Lord'. What is meant by this command? How does a person go about loving his neighbour? Does the command imply that he must love himself? Does it imply that he should love God, or that God loves him? We shall see how rabbinical interpretation found precise rules to be followed by the person fulfilling the command to 'love': theirs was not a world of vague, unlimited, concepts.

The Gospels

Reading the Gospels also requires skills, and presents difficulties for many. For Christians, their very familiarity can be a stumbling-block to new insights: for Jews, the uncomplimentary references to Jews and to rabbinic figures are a major difficulty. In compiling this work, it has been found necessary to adopt a stance on some controversial issues. In approaching the reading of the Gospel texts, the reader is advised not to regard them as mainly a record of historical fact. The reader will not find a list of dates in the life of Jesus in the Gospels, nor even a complete list of his teachings. Rather, each Gospel presents the understanding of one person or group of the significance of Jesus in his own life, the essence of Jesus as understood and accepted by those who believed in and followed him. The Gospels can thus be regarded as a kind of commentary on Jesus' life, in much the same way as the Rabbis comment on biblical texts. What is central to the Gospel writers is the experience of resurrection: the feeling that there was some-thing more in their lives than could be explained by their own resources. And what is central to the rabbinic texts is the experience of revelation, the feeling that God's will is known and available to be derived from the text of Torah.

Because the Gospels are a personal commentary, the context of a Gospel story can be very important. This is especially true in Matthew, (the Gospel most often used for this work) who clearly adopts a very careful pattern in the arrangement of his material. The thematic presentation of these units has a major disadvantage in taking Gospel passages out of context. The reader is advised to take contexts into account, and the place of the story in the plan of the Gospel.

This work is based on primary sources. All secondary material is very limited and highly selective, including the discussions of the texts contained herein. There is no substitute for direct examina-tion of the primary sources. This work differs from other works in this field in aiming to supply the reader with some of the skills necessary to go 'back to the sources'. One other skill that may well be necessary to learn is that of study with a partner or in a group: for this involves dialogue, and it is through dialogue that we discover ourselves.

Our first text is a comment on Leviticus 19.18 'You shall love your neighbour as yourself: I am the Lord.'

1 *Sifra on Leviticus 19.18*

'And you shall love your neighbour as yourself.' Rabbi Akiva says, This is a great principle in the Torah. Ben Azzai says 'This is the book of the generations of Adam' (Gen. 5.1) – this is an even greater principle.

The first comment in our *Sifra* passage is attributed to Rabbi Akiva, whose name occurs frequently in this guide. We know little about his early life: according to legend he came to the study of Judaism quite late in life: he came to be the most important scholar of his time: and he died for his faith, being martyred by the Romans in about 132 CE, at the time of the Bar Kokhba War. His obscure origins, his poverty and his martyrdom make an interesting rabbinic parallel to the career of Jesus.

The phrase translated 'This is a great principle in the Torah' represents the Hebrew '*ze kelal gadol batorah*'. The word *kelal* is frequently used in the Mishnah to mean a 'general principle', often following a list of several particular statements. Akiva does not seem to be suggesting that this is the most important principle of all. The statement means that there are many commandments (Hebrew: *mitzvot*) in the Torah which could come under this heading: for example, one should visit the sick, bury the dead, assist people getting married, and show hospitality to guests. Akiva may be including under the heading only commandments such as these which are not explicitly stated in scripture: alternatively, he may think of this 'general principle' as covering the many other commands specifically mentioned in Leviticus 19 such as helping the poor, administering justice fairly, paying wages promptly, and so on. Whichever interpretation you take, the commandment is 'general' in that it encompasses various specific duties.

Taken on its own, Akiva's statement was about 'an important principle', not necessarily the most important principle of all. The impact of Ben Azzai's statement is to introduce an element of comparison: as soon as we say that one principle is great, but another is even greater, it seems that we are after all talking about fundamental principles of ethical values, 'the great commandment'.

Ben Azzai, a rabbi contemporary with Akiva, gives us another 'general principle', which he teaches is more important. This is from Genesis 5.1: 'This is the book of the generations of Adam.'

The biblical quotation continues: 'In the day that God created man, in the likeness of God made he him.' Ben Azzai, Akiva's contemporary, seems to have chosen a very strange text as a fundamental principle. On the face of it the Leviticus statement is a command from God, whereas the Genesis verse occurs in a narrative introduction to a list of names! What kind of commandment is this? How can it be a principle of Torah? This is typical of rabbinic exegesis: the whole Torah was from God, so a command could be embedded in any verse. To try to understand it, we have to consider our next text.

Genesis Rabba 24.7 (on Genesis 5.1)   **2**

Ben Azzai says 'This is the book of the generations of Adam' is a great principle in the Torah. Rabbi Akiva says 'And you shall love your neighbour as yourself' (Lev. 19.18) – this is a great principle in the Torah, so that you should not say, since I have been held in contempt, let my neighbour be held in contempt with me: since I have been cursed, let my neighbour be cursed with me. Rabbi Tanhuma said, If you act so, know whom you hold in contempt – 'In the image of God he made him'. (Gen. 1.27).

Genesis Rabba is a much later text, compiled in early medieval times. However, this is clearly a parallel passage to our first one, from *Sifra*. The fact that the text is much later shows how rabbinic sayings could be preserved accurately in oral form for hundreds of years. In this passage the statements of Akiva and Ben Azzai are repeated in the reverse order. At the end is a comment of the fourth-century Rabbi Tanhuma, which is appended to Akiva's statement, but which really seems to explain Ben Azzai's comment. Ben Azzai suggests that the principle brought by Akiva in fact depends on his text – we must love our neighbour because we recognize that we are made in the image of God. Our function is to know the acts of God: it is from God that all the principles spring: in the fact that God created us we can understand the individual value of every human being and the common unity of all humanity. If we understand creation aright, it is logical that we must love ourselves and love our neighbour. Creation is a more fundamental principal: anyone who despises a human being, despises God: the statement 'This is the book of the generations of Adam' is telling us that this is a Torah which applies to the whole of humanity made in the image of God. (The word *adam*, as well as being a name, is Hebrew for 'mankind'.) If we must be afraid of hurting our neighbours, how much more so must we be afraid of injuring the divine image. This, says Ben Azzai, is an even higher principle.

The whole scope of the argument has thus gradually been widened. Akiva's principle contained within it various duties, but Ben Azzai's principle contains within it even more duties – both those mentioned by Akiva, and many others: both duties to the neighbour, and also to the stranger (cf. Lev. 19.34 'the stranger who dwells with you – you shall love him as yourself'). The combination with the verse 'In the image of God he made him' completes the thought. Ben Azzai's principle is therefore wider both in a halachic (legal) sense, in that it contains more specific duties, and in a haggadic (ethical) sense. The argument shows how even a very short *midrash* can require quite a complex literary analysis.

There is a Gospel passage which ends in a similar way. This is Matthew 18.10 – 'See that you do not despise one of these little ones; for I tell you that in heaven their angels always behold the face of my Father who is in heaven.' In this passage also the respect for everyone, no matter how unimportant, is linked with the idea of the presence of God, and the relationship with God. If you hurt them, you do not simply hurt a human being, but one protected and loved and in the image of God. In respecting the child, you respect God.

From the two rabbinic texts considered so far, it might appear that later rabbinic texts present a more universalistic outlook than earlier ones: but this is not necessarily the case: from our next rabbinic text a different picture emerges.

Note that the words in square brackets are words which do not appear in the Hebrew, but which have been added to make sense in English, equivalent to the use of italics in the King James Bible.

3 *Babylonian Talmud, Shabbat 31A.*

Our Rabbis have taught: Once upon a time there was a certain gentile, who came before Shammai. He said to him,
'How many Teachings do you have?'
'Two,' he replied. 'The Written Torah, and the Oral Torah.'
Said [the gentile] to him:
'In respect of the Written Torah I trust you, but in respect of the Oral Torah I don't trust you. Convert me, on the understanding that you teach me only the Written Torah.'
He scolded him, and sent him away with a rebuke.

He came before Hillel, and he converted him. On the first day [of lessons] he told him the alphabet:
'*Alef, Bet, Gimel, Dalet.*'
On the following day, he reversed the order. Said [the student] to him:
'Look here, this isn't what you told me yesterday!'
He replied:
'Won't you rely on me? Rely on me also as regards the Oral Torah.'

Again, there was once a certain gentile, who came before Shammai. He said to him,
'Convert me, on condition that you teach me the whole Torah, while I am standing on one leg.'
He thrust him away with the builder's measure in his hand. He came before Hillel, and he converted him, and said to him,
'What is hateful to you, do not do to your neighbour – this is the whole Torah – all the rest is commentary on it – go and learn!'

Again, there was once a certain gentile, who was passing behind the synagogue, and heard the sound of the scribe, who was saying,
'These are the clothes which they shall make, breastplate, and tunic.' (Ex. 28.4)
'Are these for me?' he enquired.
'For the High Priest,' they replied to him.
Said the gentile to himself,
'I shall go and convert, so that they will make me High Priest.' He came before Shammai, and said to him:
'Convert me, on condition that you make me High Priest.'
He thrust him away with the builder's measure in his hand. He came before Hillel, and he converted him, and said to him,
'Does anybody appoint a King, unless he understands the arrangement of the kingdom? – Go learn the arrangement of the kingdom.'
He went away and read, but when he reached the passage 'The stranger who comes near shall die' (Num. 1.51), he said to him,
'Who does this text refer to?'
'Even to David the King of Israel,' he replied.
The proselyte took up an *a fortiori* argument with himself –
'If concerning Israel, who are called "Children" to the Lord, out of the Love with which Scripture loves them "My son the first born Israel" (Ex. 4.22), it is said concerning them "The stranger who comes near shall die" – as for a simple proselyte, who comes with his staff and his bag, how much the more so!) He came before Shammai, and said,
'Am I at all fit to be High Priest, and is it not said in the Torah, "The stranger who comes near shall die"?' He came before Hillel, and said to him,
'The humility of Hillel! May blessings rest upon your head, for you brought me under the wings of the Divine Presence.'

Our source, the Babylonian Talmud, is a much later one, but the legend deals with the two most famous early rabbinic figures, Hillel and Shammai. Shammai (*c.* 50 BCE – 30 CE) was a leader of the Sanhedrin, one of the most important positions of his time. He became famous for the strictness of his opinions. His contemporary Hillel, of similar date, also known as Hillel the Elder, was appointed *Nasi*, (a word which means 'chief' or 'prince') quite early in his career. His appointment reflects his genius at interpreting scripture and working out the correct *halakhah*. There are seven principles for interpreting scripture attributed to Hillel, (called the laws of halachic *midrash*), and these were later expanded by Rabbi Ishmael to thirteen principles. Hillel's main activity was probably between 10 BCE and 10 CE, and he was known for the leniency of his opinions, for his humility and modesty, and for his social reforms to help the poor. It is assumed from this passage that Shammai was a builder by profession. The Rabbis of those times were not professional Rabbis, but had other trades.

There are only a few stories in the Talmud like this one, which contrast the view of Hillel and Shammai in person: there are far more disputes recorded between their followers of later generations (*Beit Hillel* and *Beit Shammai*), and these discussions continued until the end of the first century. Three hundred and fifty such disputes are recorded in the Talmud. Only very few of the names are known of the Rabbis who formed the schools of Hillel and Shammai: of those known, some of Hillel's followers were called by the title Rabbi, but none of Shammai's. One talmudic statement says that Hillel had eighty disciples, and the least (i.e. the last, the youngest) of these was Yohanan ben Zakkai.

The stories here are therefore set round about the time of Jesus' childhood, but clearly contain various legendary elements. For example, when Hillel uses the words 'Go and learn!', he uses a technical term (*gemor*) which can often refer to the study of talmudic texts – supposedly several hundred years before those texts existed!

Our text concerns three people who wanted to convert to Judaism. It is the story about the second convert, the one who wanted to learn the whole Torah while standing on one leg, which is most directly relevant to our theme of 'the great commandment'. This is a very famous story. The majority of the evidence from rabbinic times shows that on the whole the rabbis were favourable and willing to accept converts. The requirements were: circumcision (for men), *tevilah* (immersion in water), and instruction. This debate is only about the instruction element. How much do you have to tell somebody about Judaism before they convert, and how much can they learn afterwards? In the days when Jewish communities were very cohesive, a convert would naturally have lived among a Jewish community (his new 'neighbours'), and it was considered that when he went to do that he would naturally follow their ways and practices. Thus much of the detailed learning would obviously take place after he had converted, when living in a Jewish community. But there is also a debate in these stories which is about the principles of Judaism – how much does the convert need to understand these basic principles, and agree with them? Both Hillel and Shammai would have agreed that the convert is required both to understand and to accept the basic principles of the Jewish faith: the difference lay in their approach. Shammai felt the man's request to be ridiculous: there was nothing to do but send him away: Hillel felt he knew a way of explaining things briefly (It is often said that the rabbi had to stand on one leg, but in the text it is clearly the convert!) 'What is hateful to you,' he replied, 'Do not do to your neighbour.' This is connected with Leviticus 19.18, but formulated in a negative form instead of a positive one: perhaps he considered this a more practical formulation. That Hillel's dictum refers to all people, not just to Jews, is shown not only by the fact that he was talking to a non-Jew, but also by Mishnah Avot 1.12: 'Hillel says: Be of the students of Aaron, loving peace and pursuing peace, loving one's fellow creatures (Hebrew *habberiyyot* – "creations"), and bringing them close to the Torah.'

Both negative and positive formulations of this version of the 'golden rule' can be found in Matthew chapter 7. Verse 12 has a clear rewording of the positive formulation (a parallel text is Luke 6.31, and on the same theme are Luke 6.37–38; 6.41–42, and 11.11–13):

> So whatever you wish that men would do to you, do so to them: for this is the law and the prophets.

but just before that in verses 9 and 10 we read:

> Or what man of you, if his son asks him for bread, will give him a stone? Or if he asks for fish, will give him a serpent?

This suggests the same idea put in the negative way: there is just a hint in the passage of not doing wrong to somebody you care about. In many ways the negative formulation is the more practical one, because the positive formulation could lead to somebody imposing on others the things which they think they ought to like (like somebody who likes smoking and does so in a crowded room, or somebody who objects to smoking and prevents anybody else doing so). Thus the negative formulation is more constructive, viewed as a text on its own without a specific list of duties included. However, one could view the positive formulation as going beyond simply protecting the other person's interests, but doing something extra. Much of Matthew 7 is about how people relate to others, the way they are judgmental, the way they find fault with others, and what can be done about it. The general principle at the end is the one which underlies all of what precedes. Like Akiva, Jesus seems to be using the commandment as a general principle which encompasses many other commands.

To return to the rabbinic text: notice that Hillel, although he says 'all the rest is commentary', does not excuse the student from learning that commentary: a knowledge of contemporary legislation is important: the Bible does not stand on its own. This is another golden rule of rabbinic Judaism. For the Rabbis knew that the *halakhah* which they followed was not necessarily all to be found in the Bible. They had other traditions, some considered to have been given separately to Moses orally, others worked out through long-established knowledge and custom. It was the body of learning put together which constituted the Jewish practice of the day. That was true in the days of Hillel, and it is still true today, for modern Judaism remains very much the religion of the Rabbis, far removed from the religion of biblical times. Here was a man who wanted to become a Jew, and learn the Torah 'while standing on one leg'. Hillel agreed to convert him, say the commentators, because he knew that in the end he would be able to persuade him to learn everything – the 'commentary'.

The story of the first convert shows how Hillel taught the Oral Torah. *Alef, Bet, Gimel, Dalet,* are the first four letters of the Hebrew alphabet. The story suggests that one should not just accept something in writing unless there is some kind of oral explanation; Hillel proved he even knew it back to front! Here once again the importance of the correct understanding of the texts is emphasized – the texts alone are not enough. The same principle is enshrined in the Catholic Church, with regard to revelation, which exists 'in scripture and the traditions passed on without scripture.'[1] It is an element common to both traditions that revelation is not only what is written down, but what is understood within a community – a living guide, not simply an unchanging text.

The third convert wanted to be High Priest. The priesthood in Judaism was hereditary, passed down in the male line from father to son since the time of Aaron. The High Priest was, in the time of the Romans, appointed from among the priests by the Roman governor. It was therefore not possible for any other Jew, including a convert, to become a priest, yet alone the High Priest. This is a more extreme example than the first two – a man who wished to become Jewish, simply because he wanted to wear beautiful clothes: even here, Hillel was able to show him that there was much more to Torah and to Judaism than this. What he did was first to accept him, and then to send him away to learn Torah, persuading him by saying that a governor must learn what to do first; he did not confront his strange request, but worked with it.

The Temple, like the biblical tabernacle before it, was considered to be the dwelling place of the presence of God; so the High Priest, when on *Yom Kippur* he entered the Holy of Holies, was considered to come into the presence of God. For that reason there were many rules and restrictions on his state of mind and behaviour at the time. It was an important and dangerous kind of trust. The word stranger in Num. 1.51 is *zar* – which has the sense of foreigner. 'Comes near' refers to the tabernacle. Hillel explains to him that although the word means 'foreigner', and non-priest was considered to come under this category, being 'foreign' to the ritual of the temple. The proselyte clearly recognized himself as coming under this category of *zar*, and applied the verse to himself – this means that he could not possibly enter the Holy of Holies! He realized from the verse that he could not be High Priest at all.

An *a fortiori* argument is called in Hebrew a *kal vahomer* – a light and heavy. This is one of Hillel's seven principles of halachic midrash (see p. 18 above). The argument here runs like this: if an ordinary Israelite cannot go in to the Holy of Holies, how much less could I, a convert, go in. This may appear to conflict with other passages which place converts in a very high position, unless we see the argument as running like this – if the word 'foreigner' even applies to David the King of Israel, how much more clearly must it apply to me, who really comes from a foreign people.

Some aspects of the Gospel passages have already been mentioned: let us consider one in more detail. The reader should not expect direct parallels, but will notice that the same questions are posed, and the same text quoted.

4 *(i) Matthew 22.34–40*

[34]But when the Pharisees heard that he had silenced the Sadducees, they came together. [35]And one of them, a lawyer, asked him a question, to test him. [36]'Teacher, which is the great commandment in the law?' [37]And he said to him, 'You shall love the Lord your God with all your heart, and all your soul, and with all your mind. [38]This is the great and first commandment. [39]And a second is like it, You shall love your neighbour as yourself. [40]On these two commandments depend all the law and prophets.'

(ii) Mark 12.28–34

[28]And one of the scribes came up and heard them disputing with one another, and seeing that he answered them well, asked him, 'Which commandment is the first of all?' [29]Jesus answered, 'The first is, "Hear, O Israel: The Lord our God, the Lord is one; [30]and you shall love the Lord your God with all your heart, and with all your soul, and with all your mind, and with all your strength." [31]The second is this, "You shall love your neighbour as yourself." There is no other commandment greater than these.' [32]And the scribe said to him, 'You are right, Teacher: you have truly said that he is one, and there is no other but he; [33]and to love him with all the heart, and with all the understanding, and with all the strength, and to love one's neighbour as oneself, is much more than all whole burnt offerings and sacrifices.' [34]And when Jesus saw that he answered wisely, he said to him, 'You are not far from the kingdom of od.' And after that no one dared to ask him any question.

(iii) Luke 10.25–28

[25]And behold, a lawyer stood up to put him to the test, saying, 'Teacher, what shall I do to inherit eternal life?' [26]He said to him, 'What is written in the law? How do you read?' [27]And he answered, 'You shall love the Lord your God with all your heart, and with all your soul, and with all your strength, and with all your mind; and your neighbour as yourself.' [28]And he said to him, 'You have answered right; do this, and you will live.'

Matthew's chapter begins with the parable of the invitations to the wedding feast where the guests beg to be excused, so others are compelled to come. This is discussed in Unit Three below. There follow other examples of inviting and rejecting: for example, the question of paying taxes to Caesar: then the chapter continues with the discussion between the Sadducees and Pharisees about the resurrection, which only the Pharisees accept. This in turn leads to the question of the commandment. Note carefully the question which is put to Jesus. Many people remember it as 'Which is the greatest of all the commandments!', but in fact Matthew writes 'Which is the *great* commandment', not the greatest. Akiva, it will be recalled, also spoke of a 'great' general principle, not the greatest. Here also it is not necessarily an evaluation of which is greater than the other, but rather of which would include more – which is the 'umbrella' commandment? Our next rabbinic text (pp. 25–26) is from the *midrash Sifre*, and emphasizes that the *Shema* (see p. 25) is about God's special relationship with Israel. It is noteworthy that in Matthew too our story is preceded by the words (verse 32) 'I am the God of Abraham, the God of Isaac, and the God of Jacob.'

The lawyers' question begins with the word *'Didaskale'*, which means teacher. As the text is essentially a Greek composition, we cannot easily tell precisely what Hebrew or Aramaic word might lie behind it. The word 'rabbi' is frequent in the Gospels, but a different word is chosen here. Sometimes a reader might sense something unnatural about the Greek, and look for a Hebrew or Aramaic source, but here is something which reads very naturally in Greek.

Note the phrase in Matthew 22.36 'in the law', *'en to nomo'*. The word 'Torah' in Hebrew does not mean 'Law', but in fact comes from a root which means to teach, and means a 'teaching'. The difference of translation originates with the Septuagint, which translates the Hebrew phrase *mishneh Torah* as *Deuteronomion*, from which comes the English title for the Book of Deuteronomy. It may be that the translation 'Law' in English comes from the Gospels and Christianity: the rabbinic understanding of the word 'Torah' was rather different. Note also the Greek word translated 'commandment', which is also used for a commission, somebody sent on an errand. Hebrew *mitzvah* denoted a compulsory act.

Study Jesus' answer. Note how Mark begins with the verse 'Hear O Israel', which Matthew omits. Matthew goes straight on to '. . . with all your heart, and with all your soul, and with all your mind.' This is a quotation from Deuteronomy 6.5, but the RSV translation there ends with 'might' rather than 'mind'. The word 'might' seems to be substituted by a word which means 'understanding'. Alternatively 'soul' and 'mind' could both be intended to represent the same Hebrew word *'nafshekha'*, for Luke has four words, corresponding to three in the Hebrew. 'Soul' and 'mind' could both be *'nefesh'*.

In verse 35 Matthew gives the words 'to test him'. This is also in Luke, but is not in Mark. Matthew and Luke omit the first verse of the *Shema* (Deut. 6.4), which is quoted in Mark. This may suggest that the *Shema* had been discarded as the regular prayer of the

Christians in Matthew and Luke's communities. In the quotation of the following verse, Matthew follows Deuteronomy in listing three aspects of man's love of God, while Mark and Luke both give four terms – heart and soul and mind and strength. The extra term 'strength', is added by Mark at the end, but by Luke in the middle of the verse. The normal rule in Greek is to place the more significant idea last. Perhaps the extra word and the changes in order reflect current debate among Christians as to the qualities needed to serve God.

In Matthew 22.38, Jesus answers the questioner, and actually goes beyond his question: 'This is the great and *first* command-ment.' This introduces a sense of priority.

Mark continues with a section not in the parallel texts. The answer is repeated by the questioner, but with only three terms mentioned, like Deuteronomy: he gives heart, understanding and strength. The fourth term has disappeared. At the end comes the remark, found also in the other two accounts, but in a slightly different place – 'And after that no one dared to ask him any question.' This reflects the 'testing' at the beginning – Jesus has passed the test, and shown himself a true 'teacher'. Was this 'test' relevant to the time Jesus was preaching, or to the time the Gospels were written?

Luke's passage proceeds in a different way. After our text he continues (10.29):

But he desiring to justify himself, said to Jesus, 'And who is my neighbour?'

What does the term neighbour mean? For the rabbis, thinking in terms of a Jewish community, the command to 'love your neighbour' meant 'love your fellow-Jew'. But for Luke, the answer was quite different:

Jesus replied, 'A man was going down from Jerusalem to Jericho . . .'

This introduces the parable of the Good Samaritan, after which Jesus asks (Luke 10.36):

Which of these three, do you think, proved neighbour to the man who fell among the robbers?

The answer is the Samaritan, 'The one who showed mercy.' Luke deliberately moves outside the context of the Jewish world here. In other Gospel contexts, 'neighbour' (*plesion*) means a well-disposed person, the opposite of 'enemy' (*echthros*), the ill-disposed person.

Why is Luke's view different? Almost certainly because he was writing in an environment where there were many non-Jews among the community, and many families were divided between those who followed Jesus and those who did not. In this context there was a shift in who was considered a member of the family. The point of the story is the one who showed mercy, regardless of who he was or where he came from.

In bringing into the discussion quotations from Deuteronomy 6, the Gospels are including another element very important to rabbinic thinking – the *Shema*. In rabbinic Judaism, the words of Deuteronomy 6.4–9, together with two other paragraphs from the Torah are collectively known as the *Shema*: the three sections were considered important enough to be recited twice every day, as part of the morning and evening prayers. Reciting the *Shema* is sometimes called in rabbinic literature 'accepting the yoke of the kingdom of heaven' – a recognition of the importance of the concepts contained in the *Shema*, ideas which sum up the essence of the entire Torah. Our next text is an example of rabbinic thinking on the *Shema*. It is a midrashic comment on the first line of the *Shema*, (Deut. 6.4): 'Hear, O Israel, the Lord is our God, the Lord is One.' Mark's text (12.29) gave these words as an example of a 'great commandment'.

Sifre on Deuteronomy 6.4 (The Shema)   **5**

When Jacob our father departed from the world, he called to his sons and reproved every single one of them individually, as it is said (Gen. 49.1–8), 'And Jacob called to his sons,
"Reuben you are my first-born . . . Simeon and Levi are brothers . . . You, O Judah, your brothers shall praise you."' After he had reproved every single one of them individually, he again called them all together: he said to them,
'Perhaps there is in your hearts a division about He Who Spoke and The World Came To Be.' They said to him,
'*Shema* – Hear, O Israel our Father, just as there is no division in your heart, so there is none in ours about "He Who Spoke and The World Came To Be", but The Lord is our God, the Lord is One.' . . .
'Hear, O Israel' (Deut. 6.4). From this text they said that somebody who

recites the *Shema* so that his ear cannot hear it has not fulfilled his duty.*

'The Lord is our God.' Why is this said, seeing that it goes on to say 'The Lord is One'? What does the text mean when it says 'our God'? [It means that] with us he has a special relationship. Similarly 'Three times in the year shall all your males appear before the Lord God, the God of Israel' (Ex. 34.23). Why do I need [this phrase], when it has already stated 'the Lord God'? What does it mean when it says [also] 'the God of Israel?' – that with Israel he has a special relationship. Similar is 'Thus says the Lord of Hosts, the God of Israel' (Jer. 32.14). Why do I need this, seeing that it goes on to say, 'I am the Lord, the God of all flesh: is anything too hard for me?' (Jer. 32.27) – so what does it mean when it says 'the God of Israel'? [It signifies that] with Israel he has a special relationship . . .

Another explanation: 'The Lord is our God' – over us: 'the Lord is one' – over all the inhabitants of the world: 'The Lord is our God' – in this world: 'The Lord is One' – in the world to come: for so it says (in Zech. 14.9) 'The Lord shall be king over all the earth; on that day the Lord shall be One, and his name One'.

*cf. *Tosefta, Berakhot 2.14*
Said Rabbi Meir, 'Once we were sitting before Rabbi Akiva and we were reciting the *Shema* so that our ears could not hear it, because there was an interrogator standing before the door.' They said to him, 'A time of danger does not provide a proof.'

The phrase 'He Who Spoke, and The World Came to Be' is one of the many rabbinic ways of referring to God. A paraphrase is made necessary by the context.

Deuteronomy is set in the form of a speech by Moses to the people before he dies, during which he reviews some of the things which have happened to them, and some of the laws they must keep. The rabbis here viewed the words 'Hear O Israel' as a kind of quotation – not words made up by Moses, but a traditional saying which he himself was repeating. Not all *midrashim* are consistent: the idea in our passage is that the word 'Israel' referred originally to the person Israel, i.e. to Jacob, whose name was changed to Israel. The words, suggest the rabbis, were originally spoken by his sons to him: 'Hear, Jacob, our father . . .' So the rabbis tried to envisage under what circumstances these words might have been spoken to him. According to the Bible, Jacob did in fact make a speech to his sons before he died, given in Genesis 49, saying a few words to each in turn, and reminding some of them of their misdeeds, including, perhaps, the sale of Joseph. The rabbis are suggesting that Jacob was telling them off for things they had done wrong. They envisaged a further dialogue between Jacob and his sons, not recorded in Genesis. In this dialogue Jacob suggested to them that they had done so many things wrong in their lives because they had had some kind of disagreement with God – Hebrew *mahlokhet*, meaning a division: it is not entirely clear if it means a division among themselves or a division inside themselves. He would have regarded what they had done wrong as some kind of rebellion against God, and he reproved them with this. The story suggests that they replied to him '*Shema* – Hear, Jacob, our Father, we have no such division in our hearts, but we believe the Lord is Our God and a Unity.' Our *midrash* suggests that this was the context in which this line was first spoken.

The emphasis on God's unity by the rabbis in this passage may well reflect their own concerns. Many rabbinic passages criticize those who believed in 'two powers' in heaven – a phrase used sometimes to denote the early Christians, sometimes other groups.[2] This *midrash* emphasizes that Jacob's sons had no such concept of God.

There follows a halachic passage explaining from the text the known custom that the *Shema* must be said out loud. This was deduced from the word 'Hear' – you have to hear it! This is a very typical rabbinic way of deducing rules of behaviour from a text.

The footnote to this Text 5 brings an interesting story from the *Tosefta* relevant to this. Rabbi Meir was one of Akiva's main disciples, who survived the persecutions under the Emperor Hadrian, and was enabled to carry on the tradition. Because few survived, he became very important, and much of the Mishnah is ascribed to him. At this time, the rabbinic texts were not published: they existed only in the minds of the rabbis and in their private notes: on the survival of Meir and his contemporaries depended the survival of Judaism itself.

The word 'proof' here means 'precedent'. It is an example of how in cases of doubt one looked to the actual behaviour of the rabbis as a model to be imitated. This is called a *ma'aseh* – a precedent. Rabbi Meir asserts that Rabbi Akiva disagreed with the obligation of saying the *Shema* out loud, and brings a story to prove it – an event at which he was present. He was in Rabbi Akiva's house, and there was an interrogator outside. The Hebrew word here, *kasdor*, is thought to be connected to the Latin *quaesitor* – a member of the Roman secret police. Because he was outside, Akiva said the *Shema* under his breath: Jewish practice had been outlawed, and

Akiva would have been in danger if heard. The others disagree with Rabbi Meir: his story does not affect the *halakhah* – the *Shema* must be said out loud. Rabbi Akiva's action could not be regarded as setting a precedent; he was permitted to break the law because his life was in danger. It is a general principle of rabbinic law that when your life is in danger, most rules can be broken (this is discussed in more detail in Unit Five below).

The next paragraph gives an explanation of the first line of the *Shema*. The Rabbis believed that there is no redundant word in *Torah*; no repetition can be without a purpose. So they asked, Why does it say both 'The Lord is our God' and 'The Lord is one'? The answer given is that 'our God' means over us, or according to the alternative explanation, God in this world. Note how there are two different explanations given in the paragraph. This is very common in midrashic texts: often the second explanation is introduced by the words 'another explanation': it does not even matter if the different ideas are not consistent with each other. In case the ideas here might be thought to be reading too much into the text, the quotation from Zechariah is brought in to clinch it. It is very common in rabbinic literature to bring something from a completely different context to illustrate a point of deduction or logic or exegesis. The phrase 'The Lord shall be king over all the world' was taken by the rabbis to be a prophecy of a messianic future, and sometimes this was identified with 'the world to come'.

The Gospel passages place emphasis on the next verse from Deuteronomy (6.5): 'And you shall love the Lord your God, with all your heart, and with all your soul, and with all your might.' Mark, however (12.29), includes our verse as well. Matthew and Luke omit it. The verse which all three quote is also connected with Rabbi Akiva, as we see from Talmud *Berakhot* 61B where the verse is quoted with the comment 'even if he takes your soul from you' (Hebrew *nefesh*, the spirit of life). Even if you have to die, you must still continue to love God. The passage continues:

> At the time when they took out Rabbi Akiva for execution [by the Romans], it was the time for the recital of the Shema, and they flayed his flesh with combs of iron, yet he accepted upon himself the yoke of the kingdom of heaven [by reciting the Shema]. His disciples said to him: 'Rabbi, even to this point?' He said to them 'All my days I was troubled by this verse: "with all your soul", [which means] even if He takes your soul from you. I

said "When will it come into my power to fulfil this?" And now that it is in my power, shall I not fulfil it?' He kept prolonging the 'One', until his spirit left him at 'One'. A voice issued from heaven and said: 'Happy are you, Rabbi Akiva, that your soul has left you at "One"'.

Akiva had been accused of teaching Judaism, which had become an offence at that time. The rabbinic legend is that thirty to fifty thousand rabbis were put to death by the Romans (no doubt an exaggerated figure), and a period of semi-mourning is still observed by some during the spring, because of these persecutions under Hadrian. This takes place during the *sefirah*, the counting of the *omer* between the festivals of Passover and *Shavuot*.

Another interesting Gospel text which brings in the golden rule is Matthew 5.43–48.

Matthew 5.43–48   6

[43]'You have heard that it was said, "You shall love your neighbour and hate your enemy." [44]But I say to you, Love your enemies and pray for those who persecute you, [45]so that you may be sons of your Father who is in heaven; for he makes his sun rise on the evil and on the good, and sends rain on the just and on the unjust. [46]For if you love those who love you, what reward have you? Do not even the tax collectors do the same? [47]And if you salute only your brethren, what more are you doing than others? Do not even the Gentiles do the same? [48]You, therefore, must be perfect, as your heavenly Father is perfect.'

Matthew begins here with the remark 'You have heard that it was said "You shall love your neighbour and hate your enemy."' This remark has unfortunately led generations of Christian scholars to interpret Jesus' words to mean that this is the traditional teaching of Judaism, to hate your enemies. In fact no such statement can be found either in the Bible or in rabbinic teaching: on the contrary, it says in Exodus 23.4–5:

> When you encounter your enemy's ox or ass wandering, you must take it back to him. When you see the ass of your enemy lying under its burden and would refrain from lifting it, you must nevertheless lift it with him.

A rabbinic parallel to 'love your enemy' is Ben Azzai's statement in text 2 on p. 15 above, which emphasizes the supreme value of every human being. However, a phrase similar to 'hate your enemy' has been found in the Dead Sea Scrolls, in the context of the enmity of the children of light and the children of darkness.[3] Perhaps Jesus was referring to something current in the thought of a particular sect, or to the popular wisdom of the streets – without necessarily suggesting it was part of an official body of teaching.

One way of interpreting our Gospel text is to suggest that Jesus here was not contradicting the Torah, but suggesting that his followers might wish voluntarily to go beyond its basic demands. Shortly before our present passage we read (Matt. 5.17–18)

> 'Think not that I have come to abolish the law and the prophets: I have come not to abolish them but to fulfil them. For truly, I say to you, till heaven and earth pass away, not an iota, not a dot, will pass from the law . . .'

Jesus, then, goes on to suggest that loving one's neighbour is not enough: he asks for higher standards: (Matt. 5.48) 'You, therefore, must be perfect, as your heavenly father is perfect.'

Many have pointed out how our Gospel text places side by side 'love of neighbour' and 'love of God'. These sentiments are not directly juxtaposed in the rabbinic texts here studied, although both thoughts are already implicit in the wording of Leviticus 19.18 'You shall love your neighbour as yourself: I am the Lord.' A more explicit juxtaposition of the two ideas can be seen in the following:

7 *From the Testament of Dan (trans. H. C. Kee) 5.2–3*

Each of you speak the truth clearly to his neighbour,
and do not fall into pleasure and troublemaking,
but be at peace, holding to the God of peace.
Thus no conflict will overwhelm you.
Throughout all your life love the Lord
And one another with a true heart.

Notice how here we have another positive formulation of the 'golden rule', and one which was written down before the time of Jesus. Once again we are given a list of various rules which end with the 'golden rule', as if it is the *kelal* which covers all the details which precede it. This text comes from a pseudepigraphic work, that is to say, a work not written by the person by whom it purports to be: it purports to be written by the twelve sons of Jacob, but in fact was written in the second century BCE. This is not a rabbinic text. It is included here as a reminder that there was a very large body of Jewish literature not included in the Bible, dating from pre-Gospel times, most of which has been preserved and handed down by Christians: this work survived in manuscripts in Greek and Armenian. There are twelve speeches, one given by each of the twelve sons giving his testament, detailing what he is bequeathing to future generations as yet unborn.

Text 8 gives the story from Matthew of the rich young man who comes to Jesus with a question. Parallels are Mark 10.17–31 and Luke 18.18–30, taken with 22.28–30 and 13.30.

Matthew 19.16–30   8

[16]And behold, one came up to him, saying, 'Teacher, what good deed must I do, to have eternal life?' [17]And he said to him, 'Why do you ask me about what is good? One there is who is good. If you would enter life, keep the commandments.' [18]He said to him, 'Which?' And Jesus said, 'You shall not kill, You shall not commit adultery, You shall not steal, You shall not bear false witness, [19]Honour your father and mother, and, You shall love your neighbour as yourself.' [20]The young man said to him, 'All these I have observed; what do I still lack?' [21]Jesus said to him, 'If you would be perfect, go, sell what you possess and give to the poor, and you will have treasure in heaven: and come, follow me.' [22]When the young man heard this he went away sorrowful: for he had great possessions. [23]And Jesus said to his disciples, 'Truly I say to you, it will be hard for a rich man to enter the kingdom of heaven. [24]Again I tell you, it is easier for a camel to go through the eye of a needle than for a rich man to enter the kingdom of God.' [25]When the disciples heard this they were greatly astonished, saying, 'Who then can be saved?' [26]But Jesus looked at them and said to them, 'With men this is impossible, but with God all things are possible.' [27]Then Peter said in reply, 'Lo, we have left everything and followed you. What then shall we have?' [28]Jesus said to them, 'Truly, I say to you, in the new world, when the Son of man shall sit on his glorious throne, you who have followed me will also sit on twelve thrones, judging the twelve tribes of Israel. [29]And everyone who has left houses or brothers or sisters or father or mother or children or lands, for my name's sake, will receive a hundredfold, and inherit eternal life. [30]But many that are first will be last, and the last first.'

Notice the question: 'Teacher, what good deed must I do to have eternal life?' This is a very different type of question to 'What is the great commandment?' It is a naïve question, asking for a simplification of the law. This man seems a little like the convert in text 3 who wanted to be high priest.

But consider Jesus' reply here. 'Why do you ask me about what is good. There is one who is good . . .' Everything is now open to question. In the previous texts it was taken for granted God has given his Torah, and the questioner wanted Jesus to interpret it. But here the questioner is almost inviting Jesus to give an alternative to the Law, *his* way of getting to eternal life. Jesus rejects this way of thinking, and replies that if the man would enter life, he must keep the commandments.

In the rabbinic tradition, the question of eternal life was very closely tied to ideas of orthodoxy and heresy, as can be seen from the following text:

9 *Mishnah Sanhedrin 10.1*

All Israel has a share in the world to come, for it is said (Isa. 60.21) 'Your people also shall be all righteous, they shall inherit the land for ever: the branch of my planting, the work of my hands that I may be glorified.' And these are those who have no share in the world to come: he who says that the resurrection of the dead is not from the Torah; he who says that the Torah is not from Heaven, and an apostate. Rabbi Akiva says: Also he that reads the heretical books, or that utters charms over a wound and says, (Ex. 15.26) 'I will put none of the disease upon you which I have put upon the Egyptians: for I am the Lord who heals you.' Abba Saul says: Also he who pronounces the Name of God with its proper letters.

'Having a share in the world to come' is an equivalent phrase to 'inheriting eternal life'. The idea was not whether a person would go to heaven or hell, but whether a person would be resurrected or not. Having said all Israel will have a share in the world to come, the Mishnah then gives a fascinating list of those who will not have a share. The word translated 'apostate', *epikoros*, referred to someone who did not keep the commandments – and this links very closely to Jesus' reply about keeping the commandments. The first one mentioned is he who says that the resurrection of the dead is not from Torah – he who denies the resurrection will have no part of it. As we shall see, most scholars suggest that it was the Sadducees who are here being criticized – which would place the origin of the text before 70 CE.[4]

This Mishnah clearly reflects various debates current among Jews in the first two centuries. Can you have a share in the world to come if you don't believe in it – or if you deny the Torah is from heaven? One debate reflected here is that between the Sadducees and Pharisees. The Sadducees were known to have denied that the Torah contains the doctrine of the resurrection of the dead – the Pharisees disagreed. After the year 70, when the Sadducee party no longer existed, it was the pharisaic view which was followed by the Rabbis. In our Gospel passage the debate is also about how one achieves salvation – but the issues are different. The link between 'the world to come' in the rabbinic text and 'eternal life' in Matthew 19.16 raises complex issues of interpretation which is possible only to summarize very briefly here. Regardless of the term eternal life (which has the connotation of the successful completion of life), the man seems in fact to be asking 'How do I live in the right way?' This is precisely what is referred to in much of the Gospel usage of the phrase 'The kingdom of Heaven' or 'The kingdom of God.' It may well be wrong to regard the kingdom of heaven as an afterlife or a non-earthly kingdom – better to translate kingdom as 'Rule' – 'The Rule of Heaven' or of God, and this can be as effective here and now as anywhere else: in the 'Our Father', it says 'Thy kingdom Come *On Earth* as in heaven'. It refers to living according to his rule here and now: it seems to be assumed that somebody who does that will receive a reward of eternal life. In rabbinic literature too, the phrase 'kingdom of God' normally refers to the perfection of this world of ours, as in the third-century *Aleynu* prayer, which is said in every Jewish service:

> All shall accept the yoke of your kingdom: and you will reign over them speedily, and for ever and ever: for yours is the kingdom, and for all eternity you will reign in glory . . .

The kingdom of God here is the kingdom of God on earth, which all peoples must strive to build.

Jesus' questioner, having been told God has given the commandments, seems to want to keep only part of them – he wants Jesus to make a selection for him. He is not looking for a fundamental principle to remind him of all of them, but asks 'Which must I keep?' Perhaps a current debate also lies behind this text – but it is difficult to be certain, because there is no immediate background discussion. Matthew 19 begins with a move from Galilee to Judaea. The questions which arose there were – divorce (See Unit Six), little children, and then this. The man seems to want to keep only part of the comandments, and Jesus tells him he has to keep them all. Strangely, when he gives the list of the Ten Commandments, he does not mention the first five, the ones which relate to God, only those relating to us. Then the young man says 'I've done all this! What more do I need to do?' This is where it becomes more obvious that our text reflects a current debate, because it seems to set up various artificial questions. Where does the Law come from? How much is relevant? Do I need anything beyond it? Once again Jesus is prepared to go further than the law's demands: this time the suggestion is that he should go and sell his possessions. The young man goes away feeling very sad.

The idea of being *prepared* to use all one's wealth in the service of God is paralleled in Sifre on the Shema. The phrase 'With all your might' represents the Hebrew *meodekha*: one rabbinic idea interpreted this to mean 'With all your money'. This is not as fanciful as it appears, because *meod* literally means 'muchness', which could be taken to indicate your greatness in the world, i.e. your resources, your possessions. The Jerusalem Talmud reports that it was enacted that nobody should give to charity more than one fifth of his wealth: however, the passage continues with a tale of a man called Monobaz, who gave away everything he had to the poor, and said 'I have gathered treasures for the world to come' (cf. Matt. 19.21).[5] The Monobaz in this passage has been identified with the ruler of the Persian client kingdom of Adiabene in the second half of the first century CE. Monobaz' father Izates had converted to Judaism.

Our Gospel texts here, then, show Jesus at his most 'rabbinic', engaged in lively debate, and answering some of the same questions as the rabbis. At no point does he clearly contradict Jewish teaching, but twice he shows a willingness to go beyond it – in love of enemies, and giving away one's wealth.

Points for Discussion and Dialogue

Dialogue takes time. We should not expect too much too soon. Encounter with another faith raises questions about our own: if we are uncertain of our understanding of our own faith such questioning can be overwhelmingly difficult. The units here have been arranged in such a way that the earlier ones will lead to a recognition of some of the similarities between Judaism and Christianity: later, we shall go on to some of the differences. This unit has brought together some of the basic common elements of the two faiths, Jewish and Christian ethical principles.

The texts studied in this unit are relatively easy to understand: nevertheless the subject has raised a lot of polemical debate between Jews and Christians. Many scholars have wasted much ink and breath trying to work out – Who said it first? Is the positive or the negative formulation better? Was Jesus following Hillel? Which of them had a wider view than the other? It is not possible to answer these questions. In rabbinic literature the term 'neighbour' is limited to a fellow-Jew: but Hillel said one should love all creatures (p. 19 above), and Ben Azzai's comments in text 2 seem equally wide. Such arguments are in fact a stumbling block to progress in dialogue. Even with these relatively simple texts, for many the setting of Jewish and Christian texts side by side will be bound to raise more questions than it answers. Which text does one prefer? Who expressed it better?

One of the stumbling blocks to dialogue is a failure to understand the reactions of others. Some texts studied may be uncomfortable to Jews, others to Christians. Many Jews may be pleased to discover some of the more 'rabbinic' teachings of Jesus discussed in this unit, not realizing that this may be difficult for many Christians – for it may be integral to *their* faith to regard the teaching of Jesus as something new. It can come as a shock to realize that many teachings have clear parallels in rabbinic texts. Many Jews, on the other hand, hold the incorrect idea that the Gospel teachings can all be paralleled in rabbinic thought.

The first aim of dialogue, then, is to gain an awareness of one's own preconceptions and those of others, even when it is difficult or uncomfortable to express them. Everyone will have his or her own preferred texts, and anyone who reads with an open mind must admit that sometimes the Christian, sometimes the Jewish text expresses an idea better. But nobody can avoid asking the questions about influence and primacy. These issues have in fact been the major questions dealt with by twentieth-century scholars on our field. There are, for example, two books on the Sermon on the Mount, one by a Christian scholar, W. D. Davies, *The Setting of the Sermon on the Mount*, (Cambridge University Press 1966): and one by a Jewish scholar, Gerald Friedlander, *The Jewish Sources of the Sermon on the Mount*, (Ktav, New York, 1969, first published 1911). These books form a marked contrast, Friedlander arguing that everything Jesus says comes from a Jewish source, and Davies, equally convincingly, arguing the originality of Jesus' preaching. In fact, such attempts to 'prove' one faith better than the other serve no useful purpose in dialogue. Historically, it is very often impossible to say which ideas are earlier. On the one hand, the Gospels were compiled earlier than the rabbinic texts: on the other hand, the rabbinic texts contain a huge body of traditional material, much of it handed down for generations. What can clearly be said, however, is that both Jewish and Christian teachings reflect many of the same concerns and arose out of the same world. The texts collected in this unit are sufficient evidence of that.

In the past much debate between Jews and Christians has centred on each trying to prove to the other that their side came up with better ideas first: that their side embraces wider ethical principles. This first unit deals directly with these themes. From a scholarly point of view there does not seem to be really much difference in the meaning of the concepts discussed, and it is not possible to say 'who said it first'. In general one would have expected Jesus to follow a Jewish view – that was his environment, his people, his milieu. The surprise would be not when he said the same things, but where he came up with something different. Conversely, because of the early animosity between Jews and Christians, one would not expect Jews of this period to be greatly influenced by Christian thought. But one cannot rule out altogether either of these possibilities.

This then is a starting point: we cannot advance the dialogue if we try to prove each other wrong. We are required to wipe away the pain of centuries and the assumptions of a past when one of the main reasons for reading each others' texts was to prove them wrong.

The Synagogue

Initial point of comparison:
Historic

The aims of this unit are:
1. To show by means of an example how rabbinic texts can help us understand a simple Gospel narrative.
2. To show by that same example how the Gospels can enhance our understanding of Jewish life in the period.

There are many different ways in which one can compare a Gospel text and a rabbinic text: this unit is in the nature of a historical comparison – the rabbinic texts shed some light on the practice of the synagogue and the background to the Gospel story of Jesus reading in the synagogue in Nazareth, most fully told in Luke 4.16–30.

In this unit the reader will be introduced to a halachic section of the Mishnah. The text to be studied will demonstrate how much rabbinic literature proceeds in a logical flow from one point to the next. Unlike much Western writing however, the rabbinic authors were not troubled if their pattern of thought led from one subject matter into a completely different one: the connection between one sentence and the next may not always be obvious to the reader: it may be important, however, to work out what the connection is, in order to follow the argument clearly.

It will be seen that Gospel narratives, like rabbinic texts, make use of biblical quotation. In both cases it may sometimes happen that the quotation is given in a different form from that in many modern translations. If the reader is unable to understand the original languages, it can sometimes be helpful to compare different translations in order to gain a better understanding of how the quotation is being used. An example of some of the difficulties which can arise from different biblical translations will also be seen in this Unit.

In text 4 discussed in Unit One above, Jesus stated (Matt. 22.40) 'On these two commandments depend all the law and the prophets.' The phrase 'the law and the prophets' occurs several times in Matthew's Gospel, and each time its use is a little puzzling. It is easy to see how Jesus' remarks are relevant to 'the law', but what have they to do with 'the prophets'? The following Mishnah text makes it clear that it was customary once a week to read in the synagogue from both the Torah and the prophets. Jesus' phrase was thus probably a common one for 'the weekly readings'.

10 *Mishnah Megillah from Chapter 4*

4.1   He who reads the *Megillah* may stand or sit. Whether one reads it or two read it, they have fulfilled their obligation. Where the custom is to say a blessing, they say it; where it is not the custom, they do not say it. On a Monday and a Thursday and at the afternoon service on Saturday, three read the Torah: they may not subtract from them nor add to them, and they do not conclude [with a reading from] the Prophets. He who begins the reading from the Torah and he who completes it say a Blessing, at the beginning and at the end.

4.2   And at the new moons and on the middle days of festivals four read the Torah: they may not subtract from them nor add to them, and they do not conclude with a reading from the Prophets. He who begins the reading from the Torah and he who completes it say a Blessing at the beginning and at the end. This is the general rule: whenever there is an Additional Prayer other than on a Festival, the Torah is read by four. On a Festival it is read by five, on the Day of Atonement by six, and on the Sabbath by seven. They may not subtract from them, but they may add to them, and they conclude with a reading from the Prophets. He who begins the reading from the Torah and he who completes it say a Blessing, at the beginning and at the end.

4.4   He who reads in the Torah may not read less than three verses: He may not read to the translator more than one verse, or in the Prophets, three verses: but if these three are three separate paragraphs, he must read them one by one. They may leave out (skip) verses in the Prophets, but they may not skip in the Torah. How much may they skip? Only so much that the translator does not have to pause.

As with most mishnaic texts, a certain amount of explanation is necessary before this text can be properly understood. The word *Megillah* is the word used in rabbinic literature for a scroll containing the text of the Book of Esther. This is read in the synagogue at *Purim*, the feast the origin of which is described in that book. The principal subject of Mishnah *Megillah* is the laws for the reading of the Book of Esther on *Purim*. The tractate also deals with other synagogue regulations, such as the *minyan* (quorum) required for public prayer, the readings from the Torah, and so on: this tractate is the main source for these rules. As often, the Mishnah begins from that which is not entirely obvious, and what people would wish to learn: because *Purim* was a minor festival, it may be something which was not so clearly known about, and the Mishnah wanted to teach it: the rules about what happened on more important days would have been relatively clear, and took second place in the discussion. As is usual with the

Mishnah, the title reflects the starting point of the work, not the complete contents.

The opening words 'He who reads the *Megillah'* therefore refer to a man reading publicly in the synagogue on the festival. The word 'blessing' refers to a fixed formula of thanksgiving and praise said before or after the performance of a religious duty. After these first two sentences, the initial subject matter of *megillah* is left behind, and other types of reading are discussed. The phrase 'three read the Torah' means that the passage to be read is divided into three, one part to be read by each of them. No more or less than three persons are allowed. The references to new moons, and Monday and Thursday, show that these were days chosen for public reading of the scroll of the Torah. The new moon marks the beginning of the month in the Hebrew calendar. Monday and Thursday were chosen for public worship and reading the Torah because they were in ancient times market days, when people would come to town: there are references to rabbinical courts sitting on those days. The Torah was also read on Shabbat, both in the morning (paragraph 2) and in the afternoon (paragraph 1). It was also read on the festivals, on seven days each year – the three pilgrim festivals, known in Hebrew as *Pesah, Shavuot,* and *Sukkot,* and also on *Rosh HaShanah* and *Yom Kippur* (New Year and the Day of Atonement). The other days are the last day of *Pesah* and a festival known as *Shemini Atzeret.* In many synagogues today, the Torah is also read at the times mentioned, and also on *Purim* and *Hanukkah* and fast days, although these are not mentioned in our text.

Our text also mentions the readings from the prophets. Scholars have vigorously debated the origin of the prophetic readings, known in Hebrew as *haftarah.* One of the suggestions made is that when there were times of persecution and it was too dangerous to read from the Torah, then a reading from the prophets was read as a substitute and as a reminder of the passage which would have been read on that day. There is, however no clear evidence as to the date of this time of persecution. Most references to persecution in rabbinic literature refer to the second century CE.[1] The Mishnah text does suggest that it was not on every occasion that there were prophetic readings.

Another possibility is that on some occasions the prophetic reading was designed either to explain or to continue with the theme of the Torah reading: in some of the *midrashim* the work of the preacher was to take a passage of Torah and weave it together with some other parts of scripture: perhaps, if there was no preacher, another passage from the prophets would be read as a substitute for a sermon, to carry the interpretation of Torah further. Again, we do not know from what date this might have happened. In the Acts of the Apostles, there is a scene where Paul began to speak 'after the reading of the law and the prophets' (Acts 13.15): so as early as the time of Acts, both were read, but it is unclear if this would have been on every occasion when the Torah was read.

The words 'They may not subtract from them or add to them' refer to the number of people called to read, not to the text of the readings. Mishnah 4.1 dealt with the number who read on a weekday – three, no more and no less. 4.2 details the numbers on special occasions: on Shabbat it could be seven or more: these rules apply today, except that it is no longer customary for every person called to read his own section: instead, each one repeats the blessings before and after, and follows the text as the reader reads. The number seven is symbolic of the Sabbath, the seventh day of the week. The larger number emphasizes the importance of the occasion, and the readings on an ordinary Shabbat are the longest. On the other festivals the number is reduced – so six for *Yom Kippur*, five for the other festivals, and so on: occasions with four, and occasions with three.

The text of the blessing before the reading from the *Torah* is as follows:

> Blessed are You, Lord our God, king of the universe, who chose us from all peoples to give us his Torah. Blessed are you Lord, who gives us the Torah.

and after the reading;

> Blessed are You, Lord our God, king of the universe, who gave us the Torah of truth and planted eternal life within us. Blessed are you Lord, who gives us the Torah.

The wording of these blessings which has come down to us dates from talmudic times: it is not known what blessings would have been said at the time of the Gospels, and there is no mention in the Gospels themselves of the recital of blessings before or after a scriptural reading.

The remainder of the Mishnah text is easy to understand: but the reference to the 'translator' at the end may cause some difficulty. In mishnaic times a translator in the synagogue would translate the readings into Aramaic, the vernacular language. The phrase about the translator pausing is normally explained as follows: the reader has to stop after reading one verse or three verses so that the translator can give his translation: if the reader wishes to wind his scroll to another place, he has to complete it by the time the translator has finished, otherwise there would be a pause which would detract from the dignity and formality of the service (this is the explanation of Rashi). The word here translated 'pause' literally means 'to break off', so the text means that the reader may skip when reading the prophets, so long as the translator does not finish off his translation before the reader has found his place again.

The phrase 'read to the translator' suggests that he was to make an impromptu translation of what he had heard. The role of the translator was not simply to translate word for word but also to give explanations where necessary. Some Gospel passages seem to imply the existence of written translations into Aramaic, known as *targumim*. However, the rabbis did not permit the use of a written *targum* in synagogue worship, lest the translation be thought to have the same status as the original Hebrew scripture. The written translations also paraphrased and added explanations: it has been suggested that where the Gospels misquote a biblical passage, they are accurately quoting a *targum* paraphrase: sometimes explanations and paraphrases come into the translation which were not there in the original text. But other scholars insist that the *targumim* were not redacted until the third century.

Today, the readings from the prophets for each Shabbat are fixed according to a traditional list of passages. It is not known when this list was drawn up. Mishnah *Megillah* 4.10 lists two chapters which 'they may not use as a reading from the Prophets': of one of these it says 'but Rabbi Judah permits it'. This text implies that at the time of the Mishnah, the readings were not fixed. However, it does not follow that the person called up had complete freedom to choose what to read.

Here are the texts of the Gospel story:

(i) Luke 4.16–30   11

[16]And he came to Nazareth, where he had been brought up; and he went to the synagogue, as his custom was, on the sabbath day. And he stood up to read; [17]and there was given to him the book of the prophet Isaiah. He opened the book, and found the place where it was written,

[18]'The Spirit of the Lord is upon me,
because he has anointed me to preach good news to the poor.

He has sent me to proclaim release to the captives
and recovering of sight to the blind,
to set at liberty those who are oppressed,
[19]to proclaim the acceptable year of the Lord.'
[20]And he closed the book, and gave it back to the attendant, and sat down; and the eyes of all in the synagogue were fixed on him. [21]And he began to say to them, 'Today this scripture has been fulfilled in your hearing.' [22]And all spoke well of him, and wondered at the gracious words which proceeded out of his mouth; and they said, 'Is not this Joseph's son?' [23]And he said to them, 'Doubtless you will quote to me this proverb, "Physician, heal yourself; what we have heard you did at Capernaum, do here also in your own country".' [24]And he said, 'Truly, I say to you, no prophet is acceptable in his own country. [25]But in truth, I tell you, there were many widows in Israel in the days of Elijah, when the heaven was shut up three years and six months, when there came a great famine over all the land; [26]and Elijah was sent to none of them but only to Zarephath, in the land of Sidon, to a woman who was a widow. [27]And there were many lepers in Israel in the time of the prophet Elisha; and none of them was cleansed, but only Naaman the Syrian.' [28]When they heard this, all in the synagogue were filled with wrath. [29]And they rose up and put him out of the city, and led him to the brow of the hill on which their city was built, that they might throw him down headlong. [30]But passing through the midst of them he went away.

(ii) Mark 6.1–6

[1]He went away from there and came to his own country; and his disciples followed him. [2]And on the sabbath he began to teach in the synagogue; and many who heard him were astonished, saying, 'Where did this man get all this? What is the wisdom given to him? What mighty works are wrought by his hands! [3]Is not this the carpenter, the son of Mary and brother of James and Joses and Judas and Simon, and are not his sisters here with us?' And they took offence at him. [4]And Jesus said to them, 'A prophet is not without honour, except in his own country, and among his own kin, and in his own house.' [5]And he could do no mighty work there, except that he laid his hands upon a few sick people and healed them. [6]And he marvelled because of their unbelief.

(iii) Matthew 13.54–58

[54]and coming to his own country he taught them in their synagogue, so that they were astonished, and said, 'Where did this man get this wisdom and these mighty works? [55]Is not this the carpenter's son? Is not his mother Mary? And are not his brothers James and Joseph and Simon and Judas? [56]And are not all his sisters with us? Where then did this man get all this?' [57]And they took offence at him. But Jesus said to them, 'A prophet is not without honour except in his own country and in his own house.' [58]And he did not do many mighty works there, because of their unbelief.

Quite apart from the intrinsic interest of Luke's text, it gives a fascinating historical glimpse into the practices of the synagogue: it is in fact the earliest historical description of a *haftarah* reading. Here is a clear example of a Gospel text which can help to elucidate a rabbinic one. It does appear, as the Mishnah implies, that the reading from the prophets concluded the service.

The Mishnah states clearly that on Saturday afternoons and Monday and Thursday mornings there was no reading from the prophets: this certainly suggests that on other occasions they did conclude with a reading from the prophets. Certainly by the time of the Mishnah, which received this form at the end of the second century (although most anonymous paragraphs were attributed to Rabbi Meir, mid second century) a reading from the prophets took place on every Shabbat: the only earlier evidence is from two Christian sources, this text and Acts 13. These texts provide evidence that it was read in the first century: there is no reason to suppose that the practice at that time was any different from the later one.

Some have suggested that the words from the reading 'to set at liberty those who are oppressed, to proclaim the acceptable year of the Lord' indicate that this was the jubilee year, when all slaves were set free (see Lev. 25.8–17), but there is no evidence at all that the law of the jubilee year was kept in the time of Jesus.

The text read by Jesus is Isaiah 61.1–2a. None of the various English translations of Isaiah is identical with the text in Luke. The Revised Standard Version reads: 'He has sent me to bind up the broken hearted, to proclaim liberty to the captives, and the opening of the prison to those who are bound: to proclaim the year of the Lord's favour.' A footnote on the phrase 'opening of the prison' reads 'Or *the opening of the eyes*'. The International Version is very different: 'He has sent me to bind up the brokenhearted, to proclaim freedom for the captives, and release for the prisoners, and to proclaim the year of the Lord's favour.' This is the Jewish Publication Society of America's 1917 version: 'He has sent me to bind up the broken hearted, to proclaim liberty to the captives, and the opening of the eyes to them that are bound: to proclaim the year of the Lord's good pleasure.' The controversial phrase is, in the Hebrew, *la'asurim pekah koah*. The verb *pekah* which means to open, is normally only used of opening the eyes: here it is combined with the adjective *asurim* which means bound, so there are two alternative interpretations, one to open the bound eyes (of the blind), the other to open the people who are bound, to release the prisoners. Luke seems to be giving both ways of interpreting the text 'to proclaim release to the captives and the recovering of sight to the blind, to set at liberty those who are oppressed.' This last phrase is not found in the Septuagint, which otherwise Luke follows closely, except that he omits the phrase 'to bind up the broken hearted'. In the Mishnah text it is stated that it is permissible to 'skip' when reading from the prophets: and some scholars have tried to connect this with Luke's omission of a phrase here. Probably, however, the Mishnah refers to skipping complete verses.

If Luke's text is compared with the other versions, it is easy to see how much detail he has filled in for himself, making a kind of commentary or *midrash* on the outline given by Mark. The older Gospel states how Jesus went to teach in the synagogue, and that they wondered how he had acquired his wisdom. One of the questions which any homilist would ask is 'What was his text: what was he saying?' This is precisely the material Luke adds, not just as a matter of idle curiosity, but just like a writer of *midrash* attempting to link ideas to scriptural texts. Why Isaiah? One possibility is that this is evidence of a set reading: it is unclear from the Greek whether he was reading a passage given to him, or if he had picked it out for himself: the word in Greek depends on which manuscript you follow: most read 'unrolled' the book, as one would a scroll. Normally one would expect the roll to be closed at the point of the end of the last reading and the beginning of the next reading: or perhaps he opened it and found that passage. Alternatively, if it was a small scroll, which would have been wound on to one roll, the person in charge would have found the place ready for him beforehand: he would then close it, hand it to the reader, who would then open it at the place, as Luke says, and then begin. If you look at the narrative closely it does say – he was given it – he opened it – he found the place. The place may well have been fixed beforehand. This is the interpretation given by Israel Abrahams. The Greek word used for 'found' could mean that there it was, or it could mean that he looked for it and sought it out: so all the indications are unclear: except that it is very obvious that this particular quotation from Isaiah is exactly what Luke says this whole episode is about: he sums it up by saying 'Today, this scripture has been fulfilled in your hearing.' This seems rather brief for a sermon, but note that the phrase translated 'he began to say' is a Greek imperfect which could mean simply that 'he was talking to them'.

Verse 20 in Luke is also very interesting: 'the eyes of all in the synagogue were fixed on him'. But this is before he said anything! Perhaps it shows that the person who read the *haftarah* was expected to give some kind of sermon or talk: and Talmudic references show that Jewish preachers were in the custom of sitting down to deliver a sermon: in Acts, by contrast, Paul stands up to talk.

What was it about his 'wisdom' that people would have found so shocking? The Isaiah passage is a messianic one, and Luke presents Jesus as saying therefore that he is the Messiah: but at this point in Luke's narrative there is strangely no reaction whatsoever, except that they all wonder! It is only later on when he goes on to the second midrashic element – Elijah and Elisha – that there is a hostile reaction. So what is it that causes the offence then, but not before?

One way to read the text is that the people greatly wondered when he proclaimed himself the Messiah, but when Jesus came to his second '*midrash*', meaning 'the foreigner is going to benefit from this rather than you', they grew angry. The references to Zarephath and Naaman are quoted to show that Elijah and Elisha both assisted gentiles in preference to Jews. It seems that Jesus actually provokes the opposition, speaking in a way bound to cause a hostile reaction: as a scene in a synagogue, this part of the narrative appears to be unrealistic: but if we see it as a midrashic attempt to link the Christian belief in Jesus as the Messiah with the sense of opposition and rejection in the church felt by Luke's community, then our text can be read as an interpretation of this hostility within the church. This would fit with the theory that Luke was writing for people within the Hebrew tradition trying to explain the admission of gentiles to the church. The Christians of Jewish background, suggests Luke, were wrong in rejecting them. It was not Jesus' messianic claims that *they* would have found shocking, but the idea that Jesus' message was addressed to gentiles.

Another feature of the text which may reflect the attitudes of Luke's community is the opening sentence, 'he came to Nazareth, where he had been brought up'. Luke emphasizes at several points that Jesus came from Nazareth: Matthew, on the other hand, says the family originally lived in Bethlehem: perhaps the various Christian communities held different beliefs about where the family came from.[2] Luke here reminds us of this, as well as emphasizing that this is the home territory where he is going to be rejected.

Who is it who is rejecting Jesus? In Matthew and Mark they are people close to Jesus' own family, who know the names of all his brothers. They know his family: they do not believe such a boy could be so clever. Luke, by contrast, omits the names of all the brothers, substituting simply 'Is not this Joseph's son?' The people do not take offence because they know his family, but because of what Jesus actually says. Perhaps Luke is trying to suggest that the hostility to Jesus was not just from those who knew his family, but from the whole Jewish people: 'No prophet is acceptable in his own *country*.' Notice too that Luke drops the reference to Jesus' 'wisdom' to be found in the other two accounts.

In verse 23 Luke mentions the phrase 'Physician heal yourself', which he calls a proverb. There is no known source for this proverb: perhaps it was a popular saying, like 'hate your enemy' (see p. 29 above). In the Letter to the Colossians, Luke is described as a physician, so perhaps this was a personal touch added by him. In its context the saying means 'Heal your own people, heal Nazareth': it sets the scene for the harsh rejection of Jesus which follows.

There is no doubt that the rift between Jews and Christians was to widen still further in the centuries which followed. Normally, only the Christian polemical texts survive: there are relatively few direct references to Christians in rabbinic texts. However, in the case of this text from Luke, there does seem to have been a Jewish response. Many of the later fixed list of prophetic readings are taken from Isaiah. These include the whole of chapter 60 of Isaiah, and the second half of chapter 61. However, the first half of chapter 61 is never read in the synagogue service, and nor are other passages from Isaiah associated with Jesus. These omissions must have been deliberate. The Jewish response was – silence.

In Luke, then, it is Jesus who provokes the angry response from the people: but how should one understand Matthew and Mark? Is there a rational explanation there for the people's anger? Why are the family names mentioned? Was it to establish the later authority of James the brother of Jesus in the early church? The people take offence, and yet they recognize his remarks as something good, 'wisdom and mighty works'. Perhaps it was precisely because the episode in Matthew and Mark is so puzzling that Luke gave more details about it. Perhaps the evangelists were in different ways trying to account for the rejection of Israel. Luke, often the most conciliatory, is here the most polemical.

Luke also omits the reference to the family in the phrase 'A prophet is not without honour', or, as he puts it, 'No prophet is acceptable' (verse 24). The wording in the other Gospels gives the impression that there are places in which a prophet is honoured, but Luke's version is much truer to the accounts of the Hebrew prophets, that they were respected nowhere in their own time – no prophet is acceptable. For example, Amos preached in the North, but his message was not accepted even there: Jeremiah was thrown into a pit: they constantly experienced rejection and frustration.

Another puzzling aspect of Luke's text is the ending, where the crowd try to throw Jesus from the top of the hill. In the days of the Temple, this is what was done with the scapegoat. The scapegoat on which the sins of Israel were placed was let loose in the wilderness, according to Leviticus: but Mishnah *Yoma* describes how in Temple times they did not actually let it go, but led it up to a high place outside Jerusalem and dropped it over the top of a cliff. Perhaps this should be associated with the frequently recorded saying when Jesus healed people: 'Your sins are forgiven you.' It says in the text that in Nazareth he was not accepted: elsewhere he forgave people's sins, but here he did not forgive people's sins: so their anger was shown by their piling their sins on Jesus, and the evangelist is suggesting that metaphorically they were making a scapegoat of him for their sins. Patristic writing sometimes referred to Jesus as a scapegoat. Others suggest that the hill here shows the method of stoning, to drop a large boulder from a height. Normally both stoning and the throwing of the scapegoat were carried out at specific sites, so the use is more metaphorical than literal. It is the idea which is supposed to be recalled.

In later times the text from Isaiah quoted by Jesus in the story was omitted from the cycle of synagogue readings: that section and the section after are both read, but not this one. Probably it was omitted because of its association with Jesus. Yet the text remains our earliest historical evidence for the reading of the *haftarah*. Our Mishnah and Gospel texts illuminate each other, but only in modern times has it been possible for Jews and Christians to study them side by side.

Points for Discussion and Dialogue

The Christian reader of this Unit is likely to be pleased at the discovery of how an understanding of the Mishnah can help us understand the details of the synagogue scene in Luke. Nothing in the Mishnah, however, would lead us to anticipate or expect what happens in the remainder of our story, after Jesus has completed reading his *haftarah*. What does the narrative mean to us today?

The ending of the story, with its implied criticism of 'all in the synagogue', encapsulates the difficulties many modern Jews have in studying Gospel texts. The terms 'synagogue', 'rabbi' and 'Jew', all of which occur frequently in the Gospels, are the terms used today: it is easy for Jews, aware of history, to identify closely with those Jews mentioned in Gospel narratives. When Jews reading such texts are aware of centuries of persecution and anti-Semitism which have happened since the texts were written, the emotional reaction is understandable. At the very least, such texts today provoke discomfort for Jews reading them, and sometimes real anger and anguish. It does our dialogue no good if we try to hide the unpleasantness which is there.

A recently published scholarly work on Luke's Gospel contains these words on the synagogue scene:[3]

> This scene . . . sums up and presents in a dramatic way Luke's theology of the rejection of the gospel by the Jews and of the divine intent to send it to the gentiles.

This interpretation, although not written by a Jew, may well be one with which many Jews feel inclined to agree: ironically, a fundamentalist Christian interpretation might also agree with such a view. For both, the text is seen as one which sets up an antagonism between Jews and Christians.

It is important, however, to try to disentangle the text itself from the centuries of Jewish-Christian hostility which have taken place since it was written. What does the text actually say? Do the Jews in the story reject the Gospel? Certainly they try to throw Jesus headlong from a hill. But why? Jesus had preached that Elijah and Elisha came not to help Israel, but people of other nations, and suggested that 'no prophet is acceptable in his own country'. In the story as told by Luke, it is Jesus who both rejects and provokes them.

A thoughtful reader, then, might well be concerned not so much by the Jews rejecting Jesus, but at his rejection of them. The choice of one group and the rejection of another is a theme which will be found to recur frequently in the texts to be studied. What implications does that have for dialogue today? Does it lead to an 'exclusivist' theology which suggests that one faith alone can be correct, and no adherents of other faiths can achieve salvation? Certainly, that is a traditional Christian viewpoint, but it is one which many now wish to reassess. How can that be done while still accepting the truth of scripture? Some who study these units may well find themselves reading texts in a new way.

The Parable and the *Mashal*

Initial point of comparison:
Literary

The aim of this unit is to illustrate how the Gospels and rabbis made extensive use of a common literary form, and to explore both the similarities and the differences in the ways it was used.

The units in this work show different methods of comparing texts. The initial point of comparison could be linguistic, contextual, substantive: there are different ways in which one can begin to compare different literatures. Here, the point of comparison is a literary genre, the parable or *mashal. Mashal* (plural: *meshalim*) is the Hebrew term, meaning likeness, comparison, or proverb: 'parable' is the nearest English equivalent. The *mashal* began in the Hebrew Bible: Nathan's parable in II Samuel 12.1–6 is an excellent example: there are many others, going back to Jotham's fable in Judges 9, where the trees speak to each other.

The reader of this unit will need to be aware of some simple aspects of literary criticism. First, it will be helpful to consider some of the ways in which a writer or preacher uses source material. The reader may wish to try to disentangle such material from the point the writer himself is making. For it is in the distinctive way the material is used, not in the material itself, that the contribution of the writer lies. Secondly, the reader may wish to reflect on the impact the texts have made through the centuries on those of his or her own faith, and on those of other faiths. Because the texts are religious texts, they have taken on an importance through history which may be quite distinct from their original meaning. Only by being aware of the issues which have arisen from the texts can the reader gauge their impact today, and the truth they hold for us.

Every reader of the Gospels is aware of the parable, Jesus' most familiar teaching device. A tale is told: a moral is pointed. The effect of the parable is to throw the question back to the listener, to provoke a different answer from before. It also throws the reader's personal situation into relief, so that every time it is read, it can mean something different. There is an important distinction between allegory and parable. In an allegory, every element in the story has its counterpart in real life, such as the allegorical explanation appended to the parable of the sower, each step having its own explanation. More often, a parable makes a single point:

one of the best examples is the parable of Nathan to David: a rich man had a whole flock of sheep, and yet he took the one sheep of the poor man. David immediately sees clearly who was wrong: and then Nathan said 'You are the man.' Many parables can be given allegorical interpretations, either by modern scholars, or sometimes in the Bible itself: yet such allegorical interpretations limit the extent to which the parable can influence the reader or the listener. Some think that the allegorical interpretation of the parable of the sower is a later addition. To summarize: a parable uses symbols to restate the premise in a new way, in terms of the listener's own experience.

There is an interesting comment made in Joachim Jeremias, *The Parables of Jesus*, a book often read as an introduction to the parables. In his introduction he makes a remark difficult to believe: he says the parables were an invention of Jesus and unknown in Hebrew thinking and writing of the time – a very extraordinary statement.[1] In complete contrast, the *Encyclopaedia Judaica* states: 'Jesus in his parables was employing a well-established rabbinic form of conveying ethical and moral lessons.' But how 'well-established' was any rabbinic form by the time of Jesus? This remains an unanswerable question. The parable was clearly not confined to Jewish and Christian literature, but was common in other ancient cultures, especially Greek. The most famous example is Aesop's Fables.[2]

In the New Testament there are thirty-one parables: some of these have similarities to rabbinic *meshalim*, but it is unusual to find similarities of substance. In the talmudic literature, there are hundreds of parables: the *mashal* was used as a teaching method, of opening the door to understanding a particular point in an argument, or a particular passage of Torah. The parables in rabbinic literature are generally shorter and simpler than those found in the Gospel narratives: most comparisons are brief, perhaps with one point of comparison, rarely with more, lasting for a few lines.

The most common theme is that of a king: the king is God and he is likened to a king on earth. Sometimes the king can be a ruler, and mankind his subjects, with Israel as the favourite subject (a common motif): sometimes the king is also a father, and Israel the sometimes wayward but beloved son: sometimes God is a husband, and Israel is the wife. So common is the motif of the king in rabbinic parables, that it is frequently used without any particular idea of royalty, and one could substitute 'man' without affecting the parable. However, some scholars believe that the stories do have their origins in real historical events concerning various rulers. This is the thesis of Ignaz Ziegler, whose full-length study, published in German in 1903, collects and categorizes the 'king' parables in rabbinic literature under headings which reflect aspects of kingship in the Roman Empire. Apart from the frequent 'king' parables, there are many animal parables, and parables from nature.

Our first text, as in Unit One, comes from the *Sifra*, the halachic *midrash* on the Book of Leviticus. The biblical text on which it is commenting is Leviticus 26.9. In this passage God details some of the rewards for the people if they keep the commands of the Torah – they will be prosperous, with full and abundant harvests, peace in the land, and their enemies will be scattered. The passage continues (verses 9–11):

> For I shall turn unto you, and make you fruitful, and multiply you, and confirm my covenant with you. And you shall eat old store long kept, and you shall clear out the old to make way for the new. And I will make my abode among you . . .

In verse 9, the word translated 'turn' has the Hebrew root *pe nun he*, the root which produces the Hebrew noun which means 'face'. It has been given various translations in our text, such as *have regard for, turn to*. It has a sense of turning to, favouring. And so the rabbis asked the question why this verb needs to be included: were not the other verbs in the verse sufficient? No word was considered redundant. What is the particular significance of this word 'turn'?

Sifra on Leviticus 26.9   **12**

'For I shall turn unto you, and make you fruitful, and multiply you, and confirm my covenant with you.' They told a parable: what is the matter like? To a king who hired many workers. Now there was among them one worker who worked for him for many days. The workers went in to receive their pay, and this worker went in with them. Said the king to this worker,

'My son, I shall turn to you. These many workers, who did less work for me, I shall give them a smaller reward. But I intend to count up for you a large sum.'

In the same way, Israel in this world were seeking their reward before God. And the nations of the world were also seeking their reward before God. And God says to Israel,

'My children, I shall turn to you. These nations of the world have done less work for me, and I shall give them a lesser reward. But for you I intend to count up a large sum.' And that is why it is said 'I shall turn unto you' . . .

This is a parable of a king and the people who worked for him, his subjects. The biblical text states that God rewards his people for doing his commands, and so the comparison to a king and his subjects is entirely appropriate. Like many rabbinic examples, this begins '*mashlu mashal*' – they told a parable. It is anonymous and impossible to date. The large numbers of *meshalim*, and their anonymity, suggest that we are dealing with a large body of legendary stories which were used by the rabbis, and given a particular significance. However, this particular parable seems to be quite closely tied to the biblical verse, and may have been composed for its present context.

The king in the *mashal* is God – but he hired many workers, not just one. These workers are the nations: many nations, not just Israel, are working for God. Judaism has since early times been aware of the existence of other faiths in the world: this text clearly delineates all the nations as God's people, working in his name. It is suggested here that although these other nations may also establish contracts with God, the distinctiveness of Israel was in establishing its covenant first. The theme of the parable is that the first will be first – will receive a greater reward. In Jewish tradition, Israel was the first to recognize the kingship of God, and to accept his commands, and this is the reason for the larger reward.

Notice how the king calls the worker 'My son'. This is perhaps a rather strange way for a king to address his worker: it implies not a king-subject relationship, but rather a father-son relationship. When the meaning of the parable is given, God says to Israel 'My children.' This usage recalls a biblical narrative in which God calls the Israelite people his son, using the words (Ex. 4.22) *beni vekhori Yisrael* ('My firstborn son Israel').

Notice how the reward of Israel is not described as a heavenly feast, or paradise, but as a sum of money. The Hebrew is *heshbon rav*, a large account. The rabbis were not afraid to use mercenary images to discuss the Jew's relationship with God. God is the employer: He gives work, and deals out the pay accordingly.

This is a typical parable in that it makes a fairly simple point – he who does the most work gets the most pay. The theme is the choice of Israel from among the nations. In rabbinic thought, the idea of the 'chosen' people of Israel means chosen to perform the Torah – *'asher bahar banu mikol ha'ammim, venatan lanu et torato'* – who has chosen us from among all peoples, and given us his Torah. (The words are those of the blessing quoted in Unit Two above, p. 42). The choice consists of the giving of the Torah at Sinai, a free gift of love: and the allusion in our verse (Lev. 26.9) to the covenant, means the covenant at Sinai. Israel, then, has a particular task to perform in the world.

The parable discusses the question of choice, God's 'turning to' the people of Israel. This could perhaps raise the question – does not God's turning to one group involve his turning away from another? The rabbinic parable says quite explicitly that the other nations will also receive their reward, albeit a lesser one. Let us compare a Gospel parable on the theme of choice:

Matthew 21.33–46 13

[33]'Hear another parable. There was a householder who planted a vineyard, and set a hedge around it, and dug a wine press in it, and built a tower and let it out to tenants, and went into another country. [34]When the season of fruit drew near, he sent his servants to the tenants, to get his fruit; [35]and the tenants took his servants and beat one, killed another, and stoned another. [36]Again he sent other servants, more than the first; and they did the same to them. [37]Afterward he sent his son to them, saying, "They will respect my son." [38]But when the tenants saw the son, they said to themselves, "This is the heir; come, let us kill him and have his inheritance." [39]And they took him and cast him out of the vineyard, and killed him. [40]When therefore the owner of the vineyard comes, what will he do to those tenants?' [41]They said to him, 'He will put those wretches to a miserable death, and let out the vineyard to other tenants who will give him the fruits in their seasons.' [42]Jesus said to them, 'Have you never read in the scriptures:

"The very stone which the builders rejected
has become the head of the corner;
this was the Lord's doing
and it is marvellous in our eyes"?

[43]Therefore I tell you, the kingdom of God will be taken away from you and given to a nation producing the fruits of it.' [45]When the chief priests and the Pharisees heard his parables, they perceived that he was speaking about them. [46]But when they tried to arrest him, they feared the multitude, because they held him to be a prophet.

Immediately noticeable in this story is an element of violence. The vineyard is well looked after, until the owner sends his servants to collect the fruit. The servants are rejected and killed. Then the owner sends his son for the fruits, because he thinks he at least will be treated with respect: but the workers think that if they can only get rid of him, then they will take possession. The underlying theme of the parable is this: who has possession, and who can get possession? The conclusion is that the King will destroy these tenants and give possession to somebody new: so here also a question is being asked about God 'turning' – but here the question is not 'Who is God turning to?' but rather 'Who is God turning away from?' Every choice of one group, it seems, involves a rejection of another. Who is unfaithful? It seems to be a polemical text. The polemic is reflected in the violent scenes described in the story.

After telling the parable, Jesus quotes a psalm. As in rabbinic *midrash*, so here, a verse of scripture, taken out of context, can give a basis for a way of behaving and understanding. The quotation in our text, from Psalm 118.22–23, is one which is common in New Testament writings: the fact that the stone the builders rejected has become the corner stone was a useful way to describe God's new choice. However, the relevance of the psalm quotation in our text is not immediately apparent. The verse says that the very stone which the builders rejected has become the corner-stone: but Jesus' point seems to be that the kingdom 'will be taken away from you' – almost the reverse idea. The most common Christian interpretation is that the corner-stone is Jesus, who has been rejected by the Jews. Alternatively, the psalm is taken to refer to the admission of gentiles to the church. Each of these two interpretations has its counterpart in rabbinic interpretation of the psalm: the parallel to seeing the corner-stone as Jesus is an explanation which says that the corner-stone is David, the author of the Psalms, who was rejected by Saul as a young man. (This is the explanation of the Targum.[3]) The parallel to the other Christian interpretation, that the rejected corner-stone is the gentiles, is to see the corner-stone as Israel, and the rejection as the exile. This explanation is favoured by Rashi.

There is a possible alternative reason for having this quotation here: Matthew begins (21.34) 'When the season of fruit drew near'. In a Jewish community, this phrase could be referring either to the season of first fruits, (Hebrew: *bikkurim*) which is the festival of *Shavuot*, or the season of ingathering of fruits in autumn, which is the festival of *Sukkot*. At both festivals, as part of the synagogue service, a group of psalms known as *Hallel* is sung, and this includes the words about the corner-stone. In the time of Jesus, the *Hallel* would have been associated principally with the ritual in the Temple: note how the Gospel writer seeks to exclude the 'chief priests and the Pharisees'. Unlike the Isaiah text discussed in the previous unit, this psalm has remained very popular both in Jewish and Christian traditions.

It is possible that the parable had a different meaning before Matthew placed it in its present context: for without the conclusion, it can be read like a Hebrew prophetic text – who is failing to keep God's standards of moral justice? Every action has its consequences: our actions determine our own fate. But in the context of our Gospel narrative, the parable seems to contain a very divisive element: who will inherit? Who will possess eternal life? There is a bitter wrangle over the rights of inheritance and possession of the true understanding of God's will. At this time, there were many new gentile Christians joining the faith, who were not being expected to convert to Judaism. It was important for Christian leaders to establish the right of the outsider to have part of the inheritance, and this is seen in terms of the rejection of the one who expected to inherit. This was a community beginning to develop a terminology around Jesus – 'Son of Man', 'Son of God'. They would no doubt have wanted to quote this parable, because they saw Jesus in the central role of the son in the story, particularly after his death. This does not mean the parable was written specifically for this context. In rabbinic texts too, we can see how a particular idea could bring to mind various quotations or stories from the past which seem appropriate. The Gospels indicate that Jesus told many more parables than the ones which have come down to us. The selection is one which fitted the interests of the evangelists.

It is instructive to compare the preceding parable in Matthew, where the debate seems to be internal to the Jewish community:

Matthew 21.28–32   **14**

[28]'What do you think? A man had two sons; and he sent to the first and said, "Son, go and work in the vineyard today." [29]And he answered, "I will not"; but afterward he repented and went. [30]And he went to the second and said the same; and he answered, "I go, sir," but did not go. [31]Which of the two did the will of his father?' They said, 'The first.' Jesus

said to them, 'Truly, I say to you, the tax collectors and the harlots go into the kingdom of God before you. [32]For John came to you in the way of righteousness, and you did not believe him, but the tax collectors and the harlots believed him; and even when you saw it, you did not afterward repent and believe him.'

The tax collectors were an unpopular group, as today. They worked for the occupying power, the Roman government, and many of them were corrupt: they not only collected what they had to, but extra as well, on which they became very prosperous. There is a text in the *Tosefta* to the effect that repentance is difficult for tax- collectors. (Text 42 below on p. 140). The harlot, on the other hand, was in a different category, as we shall see from the rabbinic comparison which follows. A rabbinic *midrash* would be unlikely to consider tax collectors and harlots in the same category.

Our previous text discussed how the vineyard was to be removed from one set of tenants and given to a different set: but this parable does not differentiate on Jewish-gentile grounds between those turning to God: rather it deals with those who respond and those who do not respond in any society. This highlights a more general difficulty with reading the Gospels, that it is often very difficult to know who is being attacked. The town of Yavneh (Jamnia) where the rabbis collected after the destruction of the year 70, is called in rabbinic literature 'the vineyard of Yavneh'. If Matthew's Gospel can be dated after 70, it may be that those who work in the vineyard are the rabbis. However, if you look at the context of the whole group of parables in this part of Matthew's Gospel, it seems rather that it is the official temple hierarchy which is being criticized, while the outcasts or those less respectable are acceptable. The criticism in the time when the Gospels are set may be a criticism of the Sadduccean group, who effectively went out of existence with the destruction. The Pharisees at Yavneh became the establishment, so criticisms previously directed at the Sadducees would now be directed against them: they are the new establishment at the time of the writing of the Gospels: so there is some confusion: some of the criticisms of the Pharisees do not seem to make sense unless one thinks of the previous temple hierarchy, the Sadducees. Some critics point out that the Pharisees and Sadducees are put together as if they formed a single group: some say the evangelists did not in fact know who these groups were.

Palestinian Talmud, Berakhot 2.8 **15**

(Song of Songs 6.2) 'My beloved has gone down to his garden, to the beds of spices, to feed in the gardens.' It needs to say only 'my beloved has gone down to his garden to feed in the gardens.' My beloved – this is the Holy One, blessed be He. Has gone down to his garden – this is the world. To the beds of spices – these are Israel. To feed in the gardens – these are the nations of the world. And to gather lilies – these are the righteous whom he causes to depart from among them.

They told a parable: what is the matter like? To a king who had a son who was exceedingly dear to him. What did the king do? He planted an orchard for him. Whenever the son did what his father wanted, he would travel around the whole world to see where there was a beautiful plant, and plant it inside his orchard. But whenever he annoyed him he would chop down all his plants.

Similarly, whenever Israel does the will of the Holy One, blessed be he, he goes round all the world to see where there is a righteous person in the nations of the world, and he brings him and makes him cleave to Israel: for example, Jethro and Rahab. But whenever they annoy him he causes the righteous who are among them to depart.

We often find that the rabbinic writings give the reader only half the quotation required: they assume a knowledge of the Bible, and a reader who can complete the quotation. Here we need to read the whole of the first two verses of Song of Songs chapter 6, which will give us the introduction and the conclusion. Here is the 1917 Jewish Publication Society translation:

> Whither is thy beloved gone,
> O thou fairest among women?
> Whither hath thy beloved turned him,
> That we may seek him with thee?

> My beloved is gone down to his garden,
> To the beds of spices,
> To feed in the gardens,
> And to gather lilies.

The International version reads 'to browse in the gardens', and the Revised Standard Version gives 'to pasture his flock in the gardens'. The Jerusalem Bible also uses the word 'pasture'. Such differences are particularly common in English versions of the Song of Songs. The Hebrew word is *lir'ot* (with the letter *ayin*), translated feed, browse or pasture. Browse is therefore used in the sense of nibbling'. The word has the same root in Hebrew as 'shepherd' and is used in Psalm 23.1 'The Lord is my Shepherd'. It means 'to put to pasture'. 'Cause to feed' sounds pedantic, but this would be a more accurate translation than the JPSA 'feed' – he is not feeding himself, but is rather a shepherd, which is why RSV adds 'flock'.

The rabbinic *mashal* points to various repetitions in the Hebrew, and asks why they are there. 'It needs to say only . . .' The Song of Songs was in our period a controversial book. After 70 CE the Rabbis at Yavneh had to decide which books were to be included in the canon of the Hebrew Bible. There was a debate about the Song of Songs, which some thought should not be included. It was eventually included, because of the allegorical interpretation always placed upon it by the rabbis, that the story of the two lovers represents the story of God's love for his people Israel. A similar allegorical interpretation is found in Christianity – of the love of the church for Christ. This interpretation, attributed to the third-century church father Origen, is thought to have been influenced by the rabbinic allegorical interpretation. Rabbi Akiva is reported to have said that all the Writings in the Bible are holy, but the Song of Songs is the Holy of Holies (Mishnah *Yadaim*, 3.5). We know that Akiva placed great emphasis on the importance of loving God, which he did even as he was dying (see pp. 28f. above).

Some phrases in the text require explanation: 'The Holy One, Blessed be He' – a typical rabbinic periphrase for God.

God's 'garden' in the *midrash* is the world. To visualize the world as a garden goes back to the garden of Eden, Paradise itself.

'To feed (*lir'ot*) in the gardens – these are the nations of the world.' The phrase, as explained above, means to pasture the flock, so the other nations are like the sheep, whereas the spices are like Israel. This also demonstrates the choice of Israel.

'The lilies are the righteous': it does not matter that they are not sheep – the principal reference is to the righteous among the foreign nations. The verb for depart is *selek* (to go up): this is an intentional reference to conversion to Judaism. Another way of interpreting this phrase is that 'depart' means 'to go up to heaven', to die: this fits with the ending of our text, that when Israel annoys God, he causes the righteous among them to depart this world.

The parable itself is anonymous, and very difficult to date. Again there is the familiar comparison to a king – this time a king who has a son. As often in Hebrew writings, it is difficult to tell to whom the word 'he' refers – probably it is the son who annoys the father here.

Israel in the story is enjoying the orchard – like the beloved feeding in the gardens. The father travelling is like the person gathering the lilies – he takes people from the world to join Israel. But when they annoy him, he causes the righteous to depart. The text is an attempt to explain why the righteous can suffer and die, and to link their departure to times of difficulty and strife among the Jewish people. There is perhaps an implication that by their death they escape the general suffering which will befall the whole community.

Particularly striking in the resolution of the parable are the two names of Jethro and Rahab. Jethro, Moses' father-in-law, is mentioned in Exodus as being with Moses just before the giving of the Torah, but he subsequently goes away and is not present at Sinai. Many rabbinic texts state that he converted to Judaism. Rahab was the harlot in the Book of Joshua who helped the spies to escape from Jericho (chapter 2) by letting them down from the wall. It says of her in Joshua 6.25 that 'she dwelt in the midst of Israel unto this day' – that is to say, in rabbinical language, that she became Jewish. This, then, is an interesting example of the harlot who was redeemed. When our passage talks about 'the righteous' of the nations, who could imagine that it would be talking about a prostitute? This is a very striking and powerful message.

Both this *mashal* and Matthew's parable attempt to explain in a profound way some of the questions asked about reward, punishment and salvation. *Both* texts accept that the repentant will receive a reward, but whereas Matthew states 'The tax collectors and the harlots go into the kingdom of God before you', the rabbinic text says that Jethro and Rahab 'cleave to Israel'. But what of those who appear to be righteous from the start? Why do the righteous suffer? Matthew's answer is to question what righteousness is: it is not necessarily what people say, but what they do. The rabbinic answer here is to suggest that the righteous are rewarded or suffer according to the standard of behaviour of the whole community: when Israel does God's will, the people are rewarded with many righteous newcomers, but when Israel does not do God's will, they lose the benefits of having the righteous among them.

Yet another text from the same section of Matthew's Gospel deals with the theme of priority among those who work for God. Here the question is posed: how much work does one have to do to fulfil his will, and achieve merit?

16 *Matthew 20.1–16*

[1]'For the kingdom of heaven is like a householder who went out early in the morning to hire labourers for his vineyard. [2]After agreeing with the labourers for a denarius a day, he sent them into his vineyard. [3]And going out about the third hour he saw others standing idle in the market place; [4]and to them he said, "You go into the vineyard too, and whatever is right I will give you." So they went. [5]Going out again about the sixth hour and the ninth hour, he did the same. [6]And about the eleventh hour he went out and found others standing; and he said to them, "Why do you stand here idle all day?" [7]They said to him, "Because no one has hired us." He said to them, "You go into the vineyard too." [8]And when evening came, the owner of the vineyard said to his steward, "Call the labourers and pay them their wages, beginning with the last, up to the first." [9]And when those hired about the eleventh hour came, each of them received a denarius. [10]Now when the first came, they thought they would receive more; but each of them also received a denarius. [11]And on receiving it they grumbled at the householder, [12]saying, "These last worked only one hour, and you have made them equal to us who have borne the burden of the day and the scorching heat." [13]But he replied to one of them, "Friend, I am doing you no wrong: did you not agree with me for a denarius? [14]Take what belongs to you, and go; I choose to give to this last as I give to you. [15]Am I not allowed to do what I choose with what belongs to me? Or do you begrudge my generosity?" [16]So the last will be first, and the first last.'

In this story, those who were paid first were not hired until the eleventh hour, and everyone receives the same. Was the householder breaking his agreement with the labourers? He says to some of them (verse 4) 'Whatever is right I will give you.' Yet his idea of the right amount was hotly disputed by most of the labourers. There seem to be two groups working on different contracts, one for a denarius a day, and one for 'whatever is right'. It seems to be the second group, who trusted him, who accepted what he gave them, but the 'first group', who had agreed on the sum, were the ones who objected. They did not object to those who came later receiving a denarius, but 'they thought they would receive more': they objected to their own agreed pay. Thus we try to impose our own terms on how God treats others: the ones who came later had an equal need to eat in the evening, and also needed the denarius. Their needs were being considered.

What does the parable mean? It is one of those introduced by the words 'the kingdom of heaven is like', and thus it raises the question of what is meant by this phrase. Is it a term which refers to what one should expect in the future, or to the present? If the reference is to the future, the parable could well be interpreted as being about repentance. The person who comes to God 'at the eleventh hour' is as worthy of reward as the person who works faithfully for him all the time. As we shall see, some rabbinic *meshalim* make a similar point. But if the phrase 'kingdom of heaven' refers to the present, it could be more simply paraphrased by the less mysterious term, 'rule of God'. The discussion here is certainly about how God will reward those who work for him: but is the reward in this world, or in some future life? And who are the groups being referred to? Does it refer to Jews and gentiles, brought later into the covenant? Is the text trying to still the complaints of the Hebrew Christian community about the influx of the gentiles? The phrase about the last being first and the first last occurs twice in Matthew, the first time at the end of the preceding chapter (19.30). There may well be a polemic going on here. Text 12, from *Sifra*, suggested that it was Israel who came first, and therefore will receive a larger reward: the first will be first, and the last will be last: Matthew, however, puts it the other way round: he seems to be trying to shift the order away from Israel, to take them away from their rabbinic first place.

Although the *Sifra* text suggested that those who received the most work will receive the most reward, there are also rabbinic texts which present a similar idea to Matthew here, that those who work for only a short time are equally entitled to a reward. The following text is a later one, attributed to rabbis of the third century CE, but a text which clearly uses traditional material:

From Palestinian Talmud, Berakhot 2.8   **17**

When Rabbi Bun son of Hiyya died, Rabbi Zeira went forward and gave the funeral oration for him, [quoting]: (Eccles. 5.11) 'Sweet is the sleep of the labourer'. It is not written here: whether he slept [little or much], but: whether he ate little or much! With whom is Rabbi Bun son of Hiyya to be compared? With a king who hired several labourers. Among them was one labourer who was particularly zealous. What did the king do? He took this [labourer] for walks, long and short. In the evening the labourers came to receive their pay, and the king gave this [labourer] the full [day's] pay just as he gave the others. At that the labourers grumbled and said: We have worked hard the whole day, and he worked only two hours and [still] received the same pay as we [did]. To that the king rejoined: This [labourer] has achieved more in two hours than you with your hard work throughout the whole day. So Rabbi Bun has achieved more in twenty-eight years in respect to the study of Torah than another proven scholar could have learned in a hundred years. . . .

When Rabbi Levi the son of Sisi died, the father of Shemuel went forward, and gave the funeral oration for him, [quoting]: (Eccles. 12.13) 'the end of the matter: everything has been heard: fear God'. To whom may Rabbi Levi the son of Sisi be compared? To a king who had a vineyard, and he had in it a hundred vines, and they would produce every single year a hundred jugs of wine. It came down to fifty [vines]: it came down to forty: it came down to thirty: it came down to twenty: it came down to ten: it came down to one – but it produced a hundred jugs of wine, and that one vine was as dear to him as the whole vineyard had been. In the same way Rabbi Levi the son of Sisi was as dear to the Holy One, Blessed be He, as all mankind.

It has already been pointed out that biblical quotations in rabbinic texts are often taken out of context. In this text the first quotation given is one where the context is important. Only half the required text is quoted: it is necessary to look up Ecclesiastes 5.12 to find the whole relevant passage: 'Sweet is the sleep of the labourer, whether he eat little or much.' The preacher wonders what his sleep has to do with his eating: why does the text not say rather: his sleep is sweet whether he sleep little or much! The commentators explain that the verse is reinterpreted to read not *shenah*, sleep, but *shanah*, learning, as follows: 'Sweet is the study of he who serves [God]; whether it is little or much, he will "eat" (enjoy) [his reward].' This *midrash* on the Ecclesiastes verse sets the tone for the sermon which follows. The quotation in the second paragraph also needs to be read with what follows (Eccles. 12.13): 'Fear God, and keep his commandments; for this is the whole [duty of] man.' It is the keeping of the commandments which seems relevant here.

How much pay should the labourer have? In the rabbinic text the man who worked for two hours receives a full day's pay. But the king has kept him from work by taking him for walks. The point of the story is similar to that made by Matthew, but with this important difference: Matthew appeared to be talking about various *groups* of people: these rabbinic sermons, however, do not explicitly contrast Israel with other nations, but one rabbi with another. The stories remain stories about *individuals*. They give a value to achievements however small they may seem, which is out of proportion to the small value we might have given them. The sermons are therefore trying to comfort the bereaved: the value of the individual's contribution is the same, however few years he has worked. Twenty-eight years may seem a long time, but Yohanan ben Zakkai was supposed to have studied until he was 120. It is not the quantity of the study, but the quality which counts. On his walks he was able to study with the king himself!

In their context, then, these parables work well. But if they were traditional stories, what was their original function? A partial answer can perhaps be gleaned by considering the second part of the rabbinic text, about the vines. Perhaps it refers to the situation of Israel in the diaspora after the destruction: at first there were many scholars, but then fewer and fewer. The rabbis tended to look back to a glorious past age, when far more people studied Torah. Thus the rabbinic and Gospel texts are addressing different questions. The Talmud text praises two rabbis for their work, but Matthew is saying something not about people, but about God and his treatment of us.

So far the chosen texts have all been parables on the theme of vineyards or gardens. The second group of parables in this unit deals with two themes: wedding feasts and the imagery of lamps and light. Both these images are important in this parable from Matthew's Gospel:

Matthew 25.1–13 **18**

[1]Then the kingdom of heaven shall be compared to ten maidens who took their lamps and went to meet the bridegroom. [2]Five of them were foolish, and five were wise. [3]For when the foolish took their lamps, they took no oil with them; [4]but the wise took flasks of oil with their lamps. [5]As the bridegroom was delayed, they all slumbered and slept. [6]But at midnight there was a cry, 'Behold, the bridegroom! Come out to meet him.' [7]Then all those maidens rose and trimmed their lamps. [8]And the foolish said to the wise, 'Give us some of your oil, for our lamps are going out.' [9]But the wise replied, 'Perhaps there will not be enough for us and for you; go rather to the dealers and buy for yourselves.' [10]And while they went to buy, the bridegroom came, and those who were ready went in with him to the marriage feast; and the door was shut. [11]Afterward the other maidens came also, saying, 'Lord, lord, open to us.' [12]But he replied, 'Truly, I say to you, I do not know you.' [13]Watch therefore, for your know neither the day nor the hour.

The element of uncertainty is very strongly expressed in this parable: but it is not immediately clear what it is about. Once again there is the difficulty of knowing what is meant by the phrase 'kingdom of heaven', and of deciding if the reference is to this world, or the next. The crisis of the story comes when the foolish maidens have departed to buy oil, and the bridegroom suddenly arrives at midnight. The evangelist makes his point by the ending – 'Watch therefore, for you know neither the day nor the hour.' This seems a very different kind of message from Matthew's other parable – 'Many are called but few are chosen' (see text 20, p. 72). This may also be connected to the theme of repentance: be prepared to meet your maker at all times, for you never know when judgment will come. A single dramatic event, perhaps death, is referred to here, but the emphasis is not on what is to happen after that event, but rather on how to live in preparation for it: the day and the hour are mentioned at the end: the story which precedes is about how to behave before that time: perhaps the 'kingdom of heaven' is already part of our lives: we must be prepared.

As we shall see, the Torah is often referred to as a lamp or a light, and this is a parable about a lamp with nothing in it. The image appears to be one of a Law with no content, or interior direction. With this interpretation, it is not selfish to refuse to share the oil, since people cannot give to others their own fulfilment of the commandments, but everybody has to fulfil them in person.

It is fascinating to compare with this parable our next rabbinic text: it is very rare to find parallels as close as this one. The text contains a *mashal* attributed to Rabban Yohanan ben Zakkai, the survivor of the destruction, and contemporary of Matthew. The parable is a comment on Ecclesiastes 9.7–8.

> Go, eat your bread with enjoyment, and drink your wine with a merry heart, for God has already approved what you do. Let your garments be always white; and let not oil be lacking on your head.

The older translations often use 'ointment' where the more modern ones use 'oil' for the Hebrew 'shemen' – their form of cosmetics.

19 *Babylonian Talmud, Shabbat 153 A*

'Let your garments be always white; and let not oil be lacking on your head.' (Eccles. 9.8). Said Rabban Yohanan ben Zakkai, This can be compared to a king who invited his servants to a banquet, but did not fix

a time. The prudent ones among them adorned themselves and sat at the door of the palace, for they said 'Is anything lacking in a royal palace?' The fools among them went to work, for they said 'Can there be a banquet without preparations?' Suddenly the king summoned his servants: The prudent ones went in adorned, but the foolish ones went in soiled. The king rejoiced at the prudent, but was angry with the fools. He said,
'Let those who adorned themselves for the banquet sit and eat and drink, but those who did not adorn themselves for the banquet are to stand and watch.'

The reader will immediately notice the following similarities to the Gospel story:

(i) Each parable contains a very strong element of surprise: you never know when the summons will come.

(ii) Each parable is about an invitation to a banquet at an unspecified time, and how to prepare yourself for it.

(iii) Each parable contrasts two groups, one which is 'wise', and one which is 'foolish'.

(iv) The banquet is in both stories preceded by a second and sudden summons (perhaps a normal device of invitations to formal parties at the time).

(v) The moral of the story is in both cases – 'Be prepared'.

There are also important differences between the two texts:

(i) In Matthew's story the feast is for a wedding, and in the rabbinic story for a king.

(ii) In Matthew, the banquet strangely takes place at midnight.

(iii) In Matthew, the bridegroom says to the 'foolish' maidens, 'I do not know you': in the rabbinic story, the 'fools' have to stand and watch the feast, an ending which might be thought rather amusing.

Another Gospel text which the reader might like to explore in comparison with Yohanan's parable is Matthew 22.1–14, and the parallel in Luke 14.16–24. This is another story about a summons from a king to a banquet, a marriage feast for his son. In Matthew's version the story has two parts: in the first part the guests refuse the invitation, and some of the king's servants are killed: so the king instead invites wayfarers from the streets to the feast. The second part of the story reads as follows:

20 *Matthew 22.11–14*

[11]'But when the king came in to look at the guests, he saw there a man who had no wedding garment; [12]and he said to him, "Friend, how did you get in here without a wedding garment." And he was speechless. [13]Then the king said to the attendants, "Bind him hand and foot, and cast him into the outer darkness: there men will weep and gnash their teeth." [14]For many are called, but few are chosen.'

This recalls the 'fools' in Yohanan's story who had not adorned themselves for the banquet: the comparison is all the more striking because it does not seem to fit with the earlier part of Matthew's story, in which the guests are gathered off the streets. How could they have wedding garments?

The reader who considers the differences carefully may conclude that our texts consist of traditional stories, which could be used in various ways to make a point by a rabbi or preacher. In each case the point being illustrated is a different one. The moral of the rabbinic parable is 'Be always prepared and ready', illustrating the quotation from Ecclesiastes. Matthew's first story (text 18) includes this moral, but increases the emphasis on the unexpected coming of the kingdom of God. The last quoted story (text 20) is more concerned with justice and right judgment.

Like the Gospel parables, Yohanan's *mashal* is linked to the theme of judgment. Chapter 9 of Ecclesiastes is associated in rabbinic tradition with *Yom Kippur*, the Jewish Day for Atonement. White is a festive and pure colour: the high priest wore white on *Yom Kippur*. The preparation is thus connected with repentance. But whereas in the rabbinic parable the distinction is simply between the 'prudent' and the 'foolish', the Gospel texts seem to be talking about the choice of various groups. Once again, there seems to be some polemic point underlying the text. Who are the groups the stories reject? Who is being chosen? The temptation to allegorize is great, but the texts themselves remain enigmatic, open to various possible interpretations.

Like Matthew, many rabbinic *meshalim* use the imagery of a 'lamp' or 'torch', and liken the Torah to light. Lights and lamps are a very important image in Jewish tradition, from the *ner tamid* (the lamp kept burning in every synagogue) to the Sabbath candles. The image goes back to many biblical passages. The source of the idea that the Torah can be likened to a lamp is in a verse from Proverbs

6.23 – *ki ner mitzvah vetorah or* – a single commandment is a lamp, but the Torah is light itself – that is to say, something bigger than the individual lamps which are but part of the light. The difference between the images of the lamp and the light is very clear in this beautiful but complex parable:

Babylonian Talmud, Sotah 21 A   **21**

And it has been taught, This is how Rabbi Menahem Bar Yossi explained the verse (Prov. 6.23) 'For the commandment is a lamp, and the Torah is light' – the verse likens the commandment to a lamp and the Torah to light: the commandment to a lamp, to tell you that just as a lamp affords protection only for a certain time, so a commandment affords protection only for a while: the Torah to light, to tell you, that just as light is a protection for ever, so Torah is a protection for ever. And it says, (Prov. 6.22), 'When you walk it shall lead you' – this refers to this world: 'When you sleep, it shall keep you' – this refers to death: 'And when you wake, it shall talk with you' – in the future to come.

A comparison – to a man who is walking in the middle of the night and darkness, and is afraid of thorns and of pits and of thistles and of wild beasts and of robbers, and also he does not know on which road he is walking. If a lighted torch is prepared for him he is saved from thorns, pits and thistles: but he is still afraid of wild beasts and robbers, and does not know on which road he is walking. When, however, dawn breaks, he is saved from wild beasts and robbers, but still does not know on which road he is walking. If, however, he reaches a cross-roads, he is saved from everything.

Notice that the theme of death is spelled out clearly in the first paragraph – in Matthew (text 18) this idea seems to be hinted at, and also in *Talmud Shabbat* (text 19): it is specific here.

The meaning of this *mashal* is not given in the text, but can clearly be worked out from the information given. The man is walking in the middle of the night: night, it seems, is this world, and in this world he is afraid of all the hazards which can come upon him. The torch is like a single *mitzvah*, a duty from God that he can perform, and this somehow saves him, like a torch, from dangers that he cannot see in the dark. However, it does not save him from them all, because the beasts and the robbers are large dangers he cannot see with only his torch. But if he has the whole Torah, which contains all the commandments, he is saved from all dangers. But he is still lost, until he comes to the crossroads. What does the crossroads represent? Is it a choice of paths, like the blessing and the curse? Probably not. Rather, the crossroads represents death, a subject mentioned in the previous paragraph: our verse from Proverbs is explicitly linked to the verse which precedes.

This *mashal* is attributed to Rabbi Menahem Bar Yossi, who lived at the end of the second century CE. The point made is much more clearly expressed than the parables considered previously, and leaves fewer unanswered questions. It makes an interesting comparison with some Gospel passages about light:

22 **Matthew 5.14–16**

[14]'You are the light of the world. A city set on a hill cannot be hid. [15]Nor do men light a lamp and put it under a bushel, but on a stand, and it gives light to all in the house. [16]Let your light so shine before men, that they may see your good works and give glory to your Father who is in heaven.'

23 **Matthew 6.22–23**

[22]'The eye is the lamp of the body. So, if your eye is sound, your whole body will be full of light: [23]but if your eye is not sound, your whole body will be full of darkness. If then the light in you is darkness, how great is the darkness!'

Text 22 talks in terms of good deeds, the *mitzvot*. The imagery of the rabbinic parable could be applied here. This text comes from the beginning of the Sermon on the Mount: it is addressed to the disciples (the 'you' is plural). Jesus seems to be drawing a distinction between the crowds he is moving away from, and the disciples who are spoken to. Compare Matthew 6.1 – 'Beware of practising your piety before men in order to be seen by them.' Some think it typical of Matthew's style that he places opposites side by side, as if saying: your goodness should shine out, but do not act for that reason. The 'light' here represents piety expressed in practical terms.

In Jewish tradition, the image of light is also used as a symbol for the presence of God (Hebrew *shekhinah*). The significance of lighting the lamps of the sanctuary as described in the book of Numbers was the bringing of God's presence to the shrine. Thus there is a double possibility of symbolism with the lamp: it can symbolize Torah but also the divine presence. This is relevant to Gospel text 23, Matthew 6.22–23. Here the lamp could represent both Torah and also the divine presence in the individual and the community. In the wedding banquet parable, everyone had a lamp, but that story did not discuss one's perception of the Law, but rather its fulfilment – is the lamp full or empty?

The texts in this unit show that not only do the Gospels and the rabbis use the same fund of stories for their parables, but they deal very frequently with the same themes. The concepts of reward and punishment, of repentance, of salvation, of judgment, of choice, have been mentioned again and again in this brief survey. These were the themes of the sermons of the time which the parables illustrate. One distinction between the way the parables are used in Gospel and rabbinic literature is that the rabbinic texts tend to link the parable to a verse from scripture, and use the *mashal* to illustrate it: this is not often done in the Gospel texts.

Points for Discussion and Dialogue

For many Christians, the study of the parable texts brings first of all the joy of realizing there is a common heritage between the two faiths, and that these known and loved stories have parallels in Jewish sources. As literary texts the rabbinic and Gospel stories can easily be studied side by side. Certainly differences will be noticed between the rabbinic *mashal* and the Gospel parables, but both derive clearly from a fund of common stories, used by the preacher to make his point.

This realization may cause difficulties for some Christian readers. Are not the Gospels original works? How is it that the different evangelists use the same parable in different ways? What point is being made? Close textual study may lead many to the conclusion that the Gospels are not so much a history as a commentary, an interpretation of the experience of resurrection as seen by the writers and their community. The evangelists wrote to try to understand why it was that there was more in their lives than could be explained by their own resources.

Jews reading the texts here for the first time may well have a very different reaction. They may well focus on difficulties of interpretation. What do the Gospel parables mean? Many of them seem to be about one group being rejected, while another group is accepted. Was it the Jews who were being rejected? Are these stories anti-semitic? What is the real historical background? And whatever the intention of the evangelists, have the stories not been used to view Jewish people as 'rejected' by Christians down the ages? Can one escape being reminded of this? Do they still have the same meaning today?

These are difficult questions: and they are all the more difficult when they remain unvoiced. If Jews and Christians do not explain to each other openly the painful feelings these texts may evoke, then further misunderstandings arise. It is all too easy, in grappling with one's own doubts and faith, to lose sight of someone else's.

For example, let us consider the endings of some of the parable discussed. Matthew in particular tends to conclude with a pithy moral. 'You know neither the day nor the hour.' 'Many are called but few are chosen.' 'The last will be first and the first last.' What do these enigmatic endings mean? Should we consider what the evangelists meant by the phrases, or what they mean to us? Or the historical background of the text before editing by the evangelists? This gives three different ways of considering each text. The debate is in fact one about literary criticism – a choice between 'source criticism' – discussion of the sources of the text, 'form criticism' (the way the text has been compiled) or 'the new criticism' – the impact of the text on the reader. The need to choose between different schools of criticism is highlighted by looking at the *mashal* and parable, since these are literary forms. Each text has sources, an editorial stage, and an impact on the reader.

It is worth bearing these terms in mind when considering how reading such texts affects dialogue between Jews and Christians. The initial impact of a text today is not based on the historical circumstances of its writing, but on our own world view. If a text talks about 'Jews' we think first of Jews today, not those of two thousand years ago. But once we have acknowledged our own preconceptions, can a historical perspective help us? Clearly it can. Time and again the rabbinic texts defend a faith already ancient, while the Gospel texts present a new one. Sometimes this difference is accompanied by an element of violence:

But whenever he annoyed him he would chop down all his plants . . .

'Bind him hand and foot, and cast him into the outer darkness: there men will weep and gnash their teeth.'

Sometimes, too, the rabbinic texts suggest that the latecomer, or somebody who has done less work, will be rewarded. Yet this normally seems to be applied to the individual penitent or convert, whereas the Gospel writers thought more in terms of groups being saved or rejected.

What kind of impact do such texts have on us today, now that both faiths can be considered ancient? Elements of discomfort remain. The theme of rejection is a disturbing one, and one we would not like to regard as having a message for our time. Yet the parable is also a form which well expresses some of the complexities of our own lives. Even with a lighted torch, the man did not know on which road he was walking. The bridegroom who arrived at midnight, the worker who turned up at the eleventh hour, the king who would chop down all the plants in his garden – all try in different ways to come to terms with the uncertainty of our world.

Introduction to Halakhah
– the Ox in the Pit

Point of comparison:
Halachic

The aims of this unit are:

1. To introduce the reader to the study of halachic texts.

2. To demonstrate how the concerns of such texts differ from those of the Gospels.

In searching for parallels with Gospel teachings, scholars have naturally chosen rabbinic texts which concentrate on ethical teachings, and on such matters as reward and punishment, salvation and repentance. Anthologies of rabbinic literature for the general reader also tend to concentrate on these areas. This can easily create the false impression that such subjects form the bulk of rabbinic literature. In fact, the main subject of the Mishnah is *halakhah*, rules of behaviour for the individual and society, in ritual, civil, judicial, and ceremonial matters. After the destruction of the Temple, the rabbis seem to have turned their attention to the close and detailed enunciation of Torah – concerns very different from those of the evangelists, and ones which are openly criticized in the Gospels (Matt. 23.23):

> Woe to you, scribes and Pharisees, hypocrites! for you tithe mint and dill and cummin, and have neglected the weightier matters of the law, justice and mercy and faith.

The rabbinic texts are certainly concerned with close details: but the close study of such detail often reveals that the concern is to work out the principles of justice and mercy in practical terms: the rabbis were committed to the belief that it is not a simple matter to say what is 'just' and 'unjust' in a particular situation. Also, they felt a need to explain how God's teachings and rules laid down in the Bible centuries earlier should penetrate and inform every aspect of their everyday lives in a very different kind of society. Thus arose the oral traditions, later collected together in the Mishnah.

Halachic texts are closely argued, and require close scrutiny. One traditional technique for studying such texts is known as *havruta*, study in pairs. Two people work with the text in front of them, trying to understand it and discuss the issues which it raises. At first, this can be a very slow process, and it is not unusual to spend an hour or more studying a few lines. The reader of this unit is recommended to try this technique if possible with the texts given here, before reading the comments which follow each text. The technique can also be used with Gospel texts, and with the other units in this work. Ideally, for our subject, such partnerships should be of a Jew and a Christian studying together: this is, however, not an essential requirement. Allow plenty of time – it takes longer than many realize. The great value of this method is that it is a technique which presupposes that it is a valid target of study to allow our own reactions and prejudices to be expressed and heard. So it does not matter if the discussion wanders off the text itself into other issues: dialogue involves allowing the primary sources to provoke reactions in ourselves.

The Mishnah deals with a huge body of Jewish religious, criminal and civil law: and these last two form as great a part of rabbinic Judaism as the more apparently 'religious' laws. Today, many think of Judaism as a religion of the synagogue and the home, but in former times, in a Jewish society, the rabbis were also lawyers for civil and criminal matters. The Mishnah, therefore, contains a whole code comparable to the laws of our own country, or to those of other ancient societies. One of the six sections of the Mishnah is *Nezikin*, which means 'damages' or 'torts', and the first text in this unit is the first paragraph of that section, from Baba Kamma, (the title means 'First Gate'). This Mishnah tractate explains the basis of the Jewish law of damages, which is based on biblical law given in Exodus:

> And if an ox gore a man or a woman to death, the ox shall surely be stoned, and its flesh shall not be eaten: and the owner of the ox shall be free from liability . . . And if a man shall open a pit, or if a man shall dig a pit and not cover it, and an ox or an ass fall in, the owner of the pit shall pay: he shall give money to the owner of them, and the dead beast shall be his . . .
>
> If a man cause a field or vineyard to be eaten, and shall let his beast loose, and it feed in another man's field; of the best of his own field, and of the best of his own vineyard, shall he pay.
>
> If fire break out, and catch in thorns, so that the stacks of corn, or the standing corn, or the field are consumed; he that kindled the fire shall surely pay for it (Ex. 21.28, 33–34; 22. 4–5).

(In the Revised Standard Version and most English translations, the last paragraph is Ex. 22.5–6.) Notice how different this text is from parliamentary legislation today. Modern laws set out the rules: ancient law codes set out examples. Our text gives a series of cases of accidents which could happen: from this, one is expected to deduce the general principles, which could then be applied to other cases not specifically mentioned. Similar examples are found in other ancient law codes, such as that of Hammurabi. This is well explained in Cassuto's commentary on Exodus. He explains clearly the relation of these laws to those in other societies.

Note the last two verses quoted, Exodus 22.4–5. The verb for 'cause to be eaten' is *bet ayin resh*, and in the next verse, about fire, the verb for kindle is also *bet ayin resh*, the same root. The one verb has two completely different meanings – to put out to graze, and to kindle a fire. Perhaps both meanings imply some kind of wandering. A pun is intended in the Bible: they are put close together deliberately: this is one feature of the way the laws are arranged in the text, which may indicate that these verses were transmitted orally, and put in this way as being easy to remember.

In rabbinic law, animals were considered to cause damage in three different ways – with their teeth, their feet and their horns. An ox which gores, damages with its horn: but it can also cause damage with its feet or teeth. A sheep was not considered to damage with its horns: but with tooth or foot only. The distinction is important, because some texts talk about the animals, and some about the categories.

The word 'mishnah', can indicate one paragraph, as well as the whole work. This is the first mishnah, the first teaching, in Baba Kamma:

Mishnah, Tractate Baba Kamma 1.1   **24**

There are four categories of damage – the ox, and the pit, and the tooth, and the fire. The ox is not like the tooth, and the tooth is not like the ox, and neither of these two (which have the spirit of life in them) are like the fire, which is not alive, and none of these (which go out and do damage), are like the pit, which does not go out and do damage. The similar aspect of all of them is that they are likely to cause injury, so guarding them is your responsibility, and if damage is caused, the one who caused it is liable to pay for the damage from the best of his produce.

The Hebrew word translated 'category' is *av*, which literally means 'father': it can also mean a 'principal category' – this implies that there are also subsidiary categories – Hebrew *toledot*. In this text, the categories in Hebrew are: *shor, bor, maveh* and *hever*: note the sound patterns *shor* and *bor*, and *maveh* and *hever*. The last term, referring to 'fire', comes from our root *bet ayin resh*: our mishnah is specifically alluding to the section of the Bible quoted, to the kind of fire which gets out of control and causes damage. The animal put out to graze does damage by eating something, hence the translation 'tooth' (literally 'to lay bare, devastate').

The 'ox' can cause damage with tooth, or foot, or horn: but which is being referred to here? Tooth and fire and pit are specific: but ox is not a category, but an animal: it cannot be referring to tooth, which is mentioned separately. Is it 'foot' or 'horn'? This is very typical of the Mishnah, that at first sight, it seems straightforward, but when one looks more closely, it becomes unclear: it is expressed in an enigmatic and cryptic way: some of the answers are not apparent from our text, but from Jewish tradition – i.e. from the later rabbis of the Talmud and the medieval Codes. In our text, most later rabbis took 'ox' to mean specifically 'foot', because other sections of the Mishnah deal with horn, and the term used for an ox which damages with its horns is always 'goring ox' not just 'ox'. So here, for 'ox', read 'foot'. If it means 'foot', why does it say 'ox'? Probably, the categories are defined as they are because of the sound, as the Mishnah was learned orally.

The ox which damages with its feet comes from Exodus 22.4 (RSV 5): the pit from Exodus 21.33–34 (an animal falls into a hole somebody has dug): the tooth is taken from the same verse as the foot, since an animal let loose can cause either type of damage. The fourth category is the fire, and that is from verse 5 (RSV 6). The Mishnah analyses the biblical text and presents it in a different way.

Sometimes the Mishnah will quote the relevant text: more often it is not quoted, and the Talmud asks 'Where does this come from?' In this case everyone would have known that the laws of damages came from this section.

Rabbinic law distinguishes between acts done intentionally and unintentionally, and in the course of explanation, both are discussed. In our text this distinction is not made, because it is not a discussion of the penalty to be imposed. For our purposes we could be talking either about negligence or malicious damage. The Mishnah discusses an unintentional act more often than an intentional one, because the law is less clear, and the Mishnah seeks to teach things we might not otherwise understand.

Having given us the four categories, our Mishnah then comes to tell us the distinction between them. Why does it need to say X when it has already said Y: The Mishnah expresses this common rabbinic thought in a kind of shorthand here. It begins with the distinction which is the least clear, that between the tooth and the ox (the foot): what is the difference?

The answer given by the rabbis was this: the foot was considered to cause damage in the ordinary way (Hebrew: *matzui*): that is to say, just by being there. But it would only do damage with its teeth if it were hungry – this was the extraordinary category. The other distinction is this: if the animal damages with its teeth, the animal gets benefit from it, but if the animal damages with its feet, it gets no benefit: and this will affect the compensation: if a man's ox has been eating somebody else's grass all day, not only has it damaged the grass, but it also has a full stomach and he does not have to feed it. That is why it has to be a separate category.

The fire is a third category, because it is not alive, an inanimate object which has to be controlled in a different way. The wind is a factor here, but not with an animal. If a gale came along, and spread the fire, the kindler of the fire is not to blame. The fourth category, the pit, has a potential for causing damage merely by existing.

There are a number of types of damage one can think of which are not included under these four categories: but all of these have a similar aspect, that they are likely to cause injury and to require guarding. Another reason why these categories may be singled out is because it could be asked 'Who is really responsible?' If a person does malicious damage, it is obvious he is responsible, but who has responsibility for an animal, a hole, or a fire? The Mishnah always selects the cases which require discussion.

The text ends by saying the damager is liable and must pay from the best of his produce, as is stated in Exodus. In the Bible the verse applies only to the animals: the rabbis applied it by analogy to the other categories as well. The Hebrew word in Exodus 22.4 can mean either 'or' or 'and' (field and/or vineyard).

Witnesses or admission or examination would be required in court. Modern Israeli law is based not on this, but on British and Ottoman law. Many of the Orthodox communities in Israel would much prefer civil law cases to be decided in accordance with Torah law, but these laws are hardly used in modern times.

The Mishnah goes on to discuss all the categories. Our next text selects one specific one, the pit:

25 *Mishnah Baba Kamma 5.5*

If somebody digs a pit in a private area and opens it into a public area, or in a public area and opens it into a private area, he is to be held responsible. If somebody digs a pit in a public area, and an ox or ass falls into it and dies, he is liable. It is the same whether he digs a pit or a trench or a cave or a channel or ditches, he is [still] liable. If so, why does it say 'pit'? Because just as a pit which is deep enough to cause death must be at least ten handbreadths deep, so also any other type must be at least ten handbreadths deep. If they were less than ten handbreadths deep, and an ox or ass fell into them and died, he is exempt, but he is liable for any injury caused.

This Mishnah attempts to answer the question, 'What kind of pit are we concerned about?' Does it mean a hole anywhere, even on your own property? The first type is one he digs in private property, such as his own front garden, but the road outside collapses into it: the digger is on his own land, but part of the hole is in a public place – it is a realistic example. The second man is digging a hole in a public area, such as a road, and a nearby garden collapses into it. The categories may well be defined in this way because the rabbis considered it important to explain the relevance of the terms public and private domain, because these were categories impor- tant in rabbinic thought: they are not mentioned in the Bible. As often happens, the Mishnah seems to limit the general law: the Talmud often limits the situation still further: by giving closer and closer limitations to interpretation, it was possible to modify the law without denying the truth of the holy scriptural texts.

In the definition of the word 'pit', the Mishnah seeks not to limit but to extend the wording of the biblical law. This is also a common device of rabbinic interpretation. The case given in the Bible is repeated; our Mishnah then goes on to extend the biblical law to cover channels, trenches, etc. A 'pit' in the Bible is an example of a kind of hole. So the Mishnah then asks why the word 'pit' is selected to represent the group. The answer concerns the concept of 'ten handbreadths': this is a common measurement for the smallest measure of an area: to give another example, a con- struction called a 'house' had to be ten handbreadths high. This is not a definition based on the likelihood of causing damage, but a definition of what a pit is in itself. If it is not ten handbreadths deep, it cannot be called by the name 'pit'. The Torah selects the word 'pit' in order to teach that any other kind of hole has to be at least as deep as that. The last sentence exempts a smaller hole for causing death, but not for injury: i.e. the exemption is from this particular law in the Torah which mentions 'pit' and 'dies', but one could still be prosecuted under the general law of damages for injury. It does not mean that an animal could not have died from a smaller pit, but that it does not come under this law.

Mishnah 5.6 illustrates one of the complexities of Jewish law, the necessity of working out precisely who was responsible in the case of a partnership. The rabbis felt that if two persons held property jointly, it does not follow that they can both be held equally responsible for acts of negligence. They wanted to consider where the blame really lay, in the belief that in most cases of neglect there is an individual responsible for that neglect:

Mishnah Baba Kamma 5.6   **26**

If a pit belonged to two partners, and the first one went away without putting a cover on it, and the second one [also] failed to cover it, the second one is liable. If the first one covered it, and the second one came along and found it uncovered [again], and failed to [re]cover it, the second one is liable. If he had covered it properly, but [in spite of that] an ox or an ass fell into it and died, he is exempt: but if he had not covered it properly, and an ox or an ass fell into it and died, he is liable. If it fell forwards because of the noise of the digging, he is liable, but if it fell backwards because of the noise of the digging, he is exempt. If an ox with its trappings fell into it and they became broken, or a donkey with its trappings and they became torn, he is liable [only] for the animal, but exempt for [damage to] the trappings. [But] if an ox that was deaf or mad or young fell into it, he is liable. If a boy or girl or a slave or a maidservant, he is exempt.

The text could indicate that the two had joined to dig the pit, or the land on which it is dug belonged to both of them. Which of the two is responsible? An example is given – the first one went away and did not cover it, and the second one leaves later, and after that the animal falls in – the second is liable. The Torah spoke of somebody who 'opens' a pit: we now learn that this could refer to somebody who fails to put a cover on a pit: a pit is one of the categories of things likely to cause injury, and so therefore it has to be guarded: and so if two people own a pit, it is the last who failed to make it safe who is to be blamed. The second case is where the first person did cover it, but the second later found it uncovered (by an unmentioned third person) and neglected to recover it – he, the last one, is responsible. The third case deals with a pit properly covered, but nevertheless an animal fell in – perhaps an extraordinarily heavy one, an ancient equivalent of a juggernaut. In this case, he is exempt. If the animal fell forward because of the noise of the digging, he is liable, but not if it fell backwards: the animal which falls forward is considered to have been frightened by the noise: but if an animal falls backwards it is considered that this was not due to the noise: frightened animals do not start backwards. The last part of our mishnah deals with the animal's trappings, for which the owner of the pit is exempt: there is no real distinction between the ox with the broken trappings and the ass with the torn ones. This is because the biblical text did not mention trappings. Note the end of this mishnah. We frequently find in the Mishnah references to the *heresh*, *shoteh* or *katan*, normally applying to people – the deaf-mute, the imbecile (intellectually handicapped) or the minor (under age). These are people who are not fully responsible for their actions: now here the reference is not to a person, but an ox in these categories. Our mishnah says this makes no difference. Somebody who permits a mad ox to roam loose, and it does damage, is held liable, but if his mad ox falls into a hole and dies, he is to be compensated for its value. The text goes on to teach about a boy or girl or a slave or a maidservant: this may seem strange: the Talmud in discussing this says though he is exempt for death in this case, there is liability to pay for injuries: the point must be that this concerns a hole which is uncovered, and it is considered that people have some responsibility to look where they are going. The text does not imply that children and slaves are of less value than animals, but rather that people have to take some responsibility for their own actions.

The next Mishnah, 5.7, begins 'It is all one whether it is an ox or any other animal falling into the pit': although the Torah says an ox or an ass, the rabbis considered these were examples: it could equally well have been a sheep.

The very next Mishnah is 6.1:

27 *Mishnah Baba Kamma 6.1*

If somebody brings his flock into a fold and locked it in properly, but it escaped and caused damage, he is exempt. But if he had not locked it in properly, and it escaped and caused damage, he is liable. If it was broken into during the night, or if robbers broke into it, and the flock came out and caused damage, he is exempt. If the robbers let it out, the robbers are liable.

It is interesting that up to this point the Mishnah has talked mainly about oxen and asses: now it suddenly switches to sheep, as the example of the animal under discussion. One wonders why – does not an ox or an ass also need to be locked in properly? Why there does it choose to discuss 'ox or ass' and here 'sheep'? Probably the Mishnah discusses the ordinary case: it does not mean that the laws of the pit do not apply to sheep, or that this law does not apply to oxen or asses, but the Mishnah deals with the ordinary case in each example. So here it prefers to teach 'sheep'.

What kind of damage is being discussed here? Clearly foot or tooth – eating, drinking, or trampling. There are exemptions for night or robbers, which are not the fault of the owner: the Talmud brings other similar examples where he could be exempt – a very high wind which blew down the fence, for example. The robbers are only liable if they bring them out intentionally, not if they escape through a hole they made in the fence. Why? Perhaps they do not know there are any sheep there: this may reflect a difference between rabbinic and modern civil law: some deliberate intention seems to be necessary here. Note how the pit and the other items were described in Mishnah 1.1 as special cases where guarding them is your responsibility: in ordinary circumstances if you break down a fence, you would be liable to pay for the fence, but not for consequential damage. Even an employee of somebody else has a responsibility to guard the hole – it is the responsibility of the last person to leave it: the case of somebody who breaks down a fence is different: there is no *prima facie* responsibility to watch the hole in a fence.

There was no form of public compensation in rabbinic law: in fact the texts do not deal with compensation so much as the penalty, the restitution, which the court handed over to the person who had suffered the damage. All fines were paid to the person who had suffered the damage.

Our text goes on to state that if you give the animals into the care of a shepherd, the shepherd enters into the responsibilities in place of the owner. He is liable in the same way.

There is some evidence to suggest that after the destruction of

Jerusalem, the Rabbis at Yavneh placed a ban on smallholdings of cattle, sheep, or goats. This may well have been because of the amount of damage done to growing crops in fields and orchards in a frail economy totally dependent on agricultural produce. So the marauding sheep of the Mishnah was not just a theory, but an everyday reality![1]

One might, however, ask what the value is of studying such law in a modern society where it is unlikely to be operated. The fact is that anybody who studies such texts soon becomes aware that after a while the actual subject ceases to matter: one would not study these texts in order to learn what to do if you dig a hole, but because the study of Torah is itself a *mitzvah*: it is even said that for this purpose we were created. The study is for its own sake: it teaches the principles by which the Torah is elucidated, and the methods of argument which could then be applied to completely different situations.

In these particular sections from the Mishnah, unusually, there are no rabbis mentioned at all: the statements are anonymous. Anonymous Mishnah was generally considered to have been formulated by Rabbi Meir in the middle of the second century CE, but we are dealing with matters which, by their practical nature, must have formed part of Jewish law long before: it is a collection of traditional material.

As no disagreements are recorded, it is impossible from the Mishnah to know how much these texts were the subject of controversy. But it is fascinating to note from the evidence of the Gospels that such subjects could form part of contemporary debate. For example, what are we to make of Matthew 15.14:

if a blind man leads a blind man, both will fall into a pit.

This sentence occurs in the middle of one of the polemical discussions with the Pharisees. It is interesting that the Mishnah does not mention a blind man falling into a pit, and who would be responsible for this.

Another intriguing Gospel text is the following, the context of which is discussed in the next Unit, on the subject of the Sabbath (see texts 33 (i) and 35, pp. 109f.):

28 *(i) Matthew 12.11–12*

[11]He said to them, 'What man of you, if he has one sheep and it falls into a pit on the sabbath, will not lay hold of it and lift it out? [12]Of how much

more value is a man than a sheep! So it is lawful to do good on the sabbath.'

(ii) Luke 14.5

And he said to them, 'Which of you, having an ass or an ox that has fallen into a well, will not immediately pull him out on a sabbath day?'

After studying the Mishnah, it is very interesting to notice that. Matthew writes of 'sheep', Luke of 'an ox or ass'. There seems to be some awareness of the rabbinic discussions which were taking place, and this colours the presentation. It seems likely that Matthew and Luke had access to the same source material: but on a number of occasions Luke seems to use a form of the text which fits better with current concerns in Jewish circles: he seems sometimes to be closer to contemporary discussions than Matthew. This, along with other internal evidence throws doubt on theories that he was himself a gentile. It is significant that we find the animal falling into the pit as a question about the Sabbath, but the matter of damages does not arise: he does not discuss the animal being killed. Perhaps that could be why Matthew has changed it to a sheep, which might be less likely to be killed in a fall than the larger animal. Matthew does mention value, but as part of a *kal vahomer*, an *a fortiori* argument, a way of reasoning much loved by the rabbis: although here and elsewhere in the Gospels the argument does not work quite as it would have done with the rabbis: if you are prepared to save a sheep, suggests the Gospels, how much more should you be prepared to save a human being.

Can the Sabbath laws be set aside to save an animal? The case here is not mentioned in the Mishnah, but is mentioned in a *baraita*, an oral tradition not included in the Mishnah but known from a later Talmudic text (*Shabbat* 128 B):

> if an animal falls into a stream of water [on the Sabbath], provisions are made for it where it lies, so that it should not perish.

In other words, it is clearly not permitted to take the animal out, but it can be provided for in other ways. This fits with our Gospel texts: Jesus' point is that they go against the law, not that they obey it.

The following Gospel text is also of interest:

29 *Matthew 18.10–14*

[10]'See that you do not despise one of these little ones; for I tell you that in heaven their angels always behold the face of my Father who is in heaven. [12]What do you think? If a man has a hundred sheep, and one of them has gone astray, does he not leave the ninety-nine on the hills and go in search of the one that went astray? [13]And if he finds it, truly, I say to you, he rejoices over it more than the ninety-nine that never went astray. [14]So it is not the will of my Father who is in heaven that one of these little ones should perish.'

Having studied the mishnaic argument, we notice some things missing here: no mention of the damage this straying sheep may have done – the whole concentration is on the recovery of the lost property, not on one's liabilities to anybody else. What are the other ninety-nine sheep doing while the shepherd is away? Note the complete difference of interest in the Gospels – the sheep as an image of something the man wishes to preserve, and the comparison with the children, as the ones who are unable to look after themselves. In the Mishnah too, the sheep are a pictorial image, but they are an example of something which causes damage: here they are an example of something precious. In both cases they are an example, but of something completely different. In this case, the Gospel text gives a more idealized picture.

This comparison may begin to suggest some answers as to what a Gospel is about – it is obviously different in character, even when quoting legal passages, from the kind of material in the Mishnah. It is in no sense a legal document, but one which uses the images of daily life in a very different way, a way which demands a different sort of response. What kind of text, then, is a Gospel? To put it simply, whereas Mishnah deals mainly with *halakhah*, the Gospels are virtually all *aggadah*, which teaches a moral diretion, not specific rules.

Points for Discussion and Dialogue

The kind of texts studied in this unit may well be new, not only to Christians, but also to many Jewish readers: the concerns of our modern world seem at first sight so different. But are they? A practising lawyer will not find them strange. Today, we tend to classify 'religion' and 'law' as separate realities which do not overlap, and we feel alienated from texts such as these, and indeed from those passages in the Bible on which they are based. We have all been influenced to some extent by those writings prejudiced against 'legalism'. Yet nothing in Matthew suggests that the laws should not be kept (see also Matt. 5.18, quoted on p. 30): it is simply that the concerns of the evangelist and his community were different ones. Our Mishnah shows that 'legalism' was concerned with real issues of responsibility and justice, and provided the basis for courts and judges to make equitable decisions.

Over the centuries which followed the composition of our texts, Judaism and Christianity grew further apart. Christianity never developed its own body of civil legislation: it was Roman law which formed the basis for civil law in Christian societies. Two caricatures arose: the Christian religion of 'faith', and the Jewish religion of 'law'. Today, under the influence of these caricatures, we sometimes undervalue other aspects of our own religious experience and faith. Need this be so?

Unit Five

Shabbat

Initial point of comparison:
Halachic

The aims of this unit are:

1. To explain the halachic background to the discussions about the Sabbath in the Gospels:

2. To compare and contrast the concerns and interests of the Gospels and the rabbis on this topic:

3. To suggest a model for dialogue which arises out of this discussion.

The reader of the rabbinic texts in this unit will notice one particular aspect of the working of the rabbinic mind. Rabbinic texts do not often begin with a problem, look at scripture, and find from that the solution: instead they seem to start from a learned awareness of what the answer is, and go on to find justification from the sources and links with the tradition. This is only a safe exercise when it is done from a very firm knowledge of and commitment to a tradition, so that the prior awareness about the answer is well-grounded: but once some understanding of the *halakhah* has been reached, its continuity with the tradition can be established through texts. A good example of this is the *Mekhilta* text to be studied in this unit, on the subject of saving life on the Sabbath.

There are several well-known stories in the Gospels in which the issue of Jesus' activities on the Sabbath is debated, and most of these concentrate on the question of healing. It is therefore relevant to look at some of the rabbinic sources, to try to reach an understanding of what was permitted and what was prohibited to be done on Shabbat in Jewish communities in the mishnaic period.

The celebration of Shabbat is first mentioned at the beginning of the second chapter of Genesis, at the end of the story of the creation of the world, where it is stated that God rested on the seventh day. In the Book of Exodus, it is stated in the Ten Commandments (Ex. 20.9–10):

Six days shall you labour and do all your work, but the seventh day is the Sabbath of the Lord, your God: on this day you shall do no work.

The word translated 'work' is in Hebrew *melakhah*. What this term means is not defined in the biblical text, but from earliest times there must have been various types of work specifically prohibited on Shabbat, handed down through families in an oral tradition. In the rabbinic period, the traditions were codified and categorized in great detail. Mishnah *Shabbat* states precisely what work was permitted, and what was prohibited on that day.

There was clearly a difficulty for the Rabbis in the fact that the Torah does not state explicitly what was meant by the word *melakhah* – work: so they looked for passages which might give some hint of God's intention. Over the centuries various traditions had naturally arisen of what the prohibited tasks were: and Rabbi Akiva connected these traditions with chapter 35 of Exodus, where Moses gives instructions for the building of the Tabernacle in the wilderness:[1] this is part of a longer section which covers all the materials required for the Tabernacle, as well as its building. At the beginning of Moses' speech, before he tells them to bring in the gold and the brass and the skins and the wood and so on, he begins (Ex. 35.2):

> Six days shall work be done, but on the seventh day there shall be to you a holy day, a Sabbath of rest to the Lord: whoever does any work on that day shall be put to death.

This passage seems out of place in this context: so it was deduced that it was there to tell the people not to work on the Tabernacle on the Sabbath: and from this the rabbis concluded that *melakhah* can be defined as all the tasks necessary for the construction of the tabernacle and the preparation of the materials – from sowing the grain to raising the animals for hides and wool. They made a list of thirty-nine types of *melakhah*, which they called the *avot melakhah* – the 'fathers' or principal categories of prohibited work. All thirty-nine are listed in Mishnah *Shabbat*, Chapter 7, Mishnah 2:

> The principal classes of work are forty less one: sowing, ploughing, reaping, binding sheaves, threshing, winnowing, sorting crops, grinding, sifting, kneading, baking, shearing wool, bleaching or beating or dyeing it, spinning, stretching it, making two loops, weaving two threads, separating two threads, tying a knot, untying a knot, sewing two stitches, tearing in order to sew two stitches, hunting a deer, slaughtering or flaying or salting it or curing its hide, scraping it or cutting it up, writing two letters, erasing in order to write two letters, building, demolition, extinguishing fire, lighting fire, striking with a hammer and carrying from one domain into another. These are the main classes of work: forty less one.

There were other types of work also which were prohibited, called by the rabbis of the Talmud the *toledot melakhah* (subdivision of work). So many and varied were the rules of Sabbath observance, that the Mishnah at one point calls them 'mountains hanging by a hair' (Mishnah *Hagigah* 1.8) – that is to say, the scriptural basis is very brief, and the rules many.

The following text begins by discussing the idea of 'rest' on the Sabbath, and goes on to consider circumstances in which life is in danger:

Mekhilta, Tractate Shabbata (on Exodus 31.12ff.)   **30**

'You shall surely keep my Sabbaths.' Why is this said, seeing that it states [earlier], 'You shall not do any work-activity' (Ex. 20.10).But from this [latter text] I know only about work activities. From where do I know about resting? This is what it means when it says 'You shall surely keep my Sabbaths', to include activities which are conducive to resting.

Once Rabbi Ishmael, Rabbi Elazar ben Azariah, and Rabbi Akiva were walking along a road, and Levi the netmaker, and Ishmael the son of Rabbi Elazar ben Azariah were walking after them. The following question was asked by them – from where do we know that the duty of saving life overrides the Sabbath? Rabbi Ishmael answered and said, 'Behold it says,* "If a thief be found in the very act of breaking in . . ." etc. Now this [refers to a case] when there is a doubt whether he came to steal, or whether he came to kill: and surely this is an *a fortiori* argument – if the shedding of blood, which defiles the land and causes the Divine Presence to depart from it, overrides the Sabbath, how much more so does the saving of life override the Sabbath.'

Rabbi Elazar ben Azariah answered and said,

'If circumcision, which affects only one of a person's limbs, overrides the Sabbath, how much more so should the whole of the remainder of the body.'

They said to him,

'From the case that you bring – just as there [it is a case of] certainty, so here [it is a case of] certainty.'

Rabbi Akiva says,

'If murder overrides the Temple service, and the Temple service overrides the Sabbath, how much more does the saving of life override the Sabbath.'

Rabbi Yossi the Galilean says,

'When it says, "But my Sabbaths you shall keep", [the word] "but" [implies] a distinction – there are Sabbaths on which you should rest, and Sabbaths on which you should not rest.'

Rabbi Shimon ben Menasia says,

'Behold it says, (Ex. 31.14) "And you shall keep the Sabbath, for it is holy to you" – the Sabbath was handed to you, not you to the Sabbath.'

Rabbi Natan says,

'Behold it says, (Ex. 31.16), "And the people of Israel shall keep the Sabbath to observe the Sabbath throughout their generations." Profane one Sabbath, [in order to be able to] keep many Sabbaths.'

*Ex. 22.1 (in most English versions 22.2).

The quotation at the start of this text is from Exodus 31.12. The rabbis asked, in a way with which the reader will by now be familiar, why this verse was necessary, since we have already learned from elsewhere (from the Ten Commandments) that work is prohibited on Shabbat. The reply is that 'keep' my Sabbaths means that 'rest' has to have positive aspects – not just refraining from work, but including activities which are conducive to rest. In later rabbinic literature, the duty to rest became known as *shevut*, and this duty was taken to include a general prohibition on strenuous activities, such as climbing and swimming, on Shabbat.

. Rabbinic literature clearly defines which activities were allowed on Shabbat. Plucking corn, for example, was prohibited under the category of 'reaping'. Healing, however, is a more complex matter to fit into the categories. It is necessary to work out which kind of *melakhah* it could come under. Certainly giving medicine was generally prohibited – this comes under the category of 'grinding', because in ancient and medieval times medicines were prepared on the spot by grinding various powders: herbal medicine would be prohibited on Shabbat because of the picking of the herbs – it was the preparation of the medicine which was at issue.

Once the prohibition of medicine was made, the rabbis applied it even if plucking and grinding were not involved. This is not mentioned in the Mishnah, but later authorities prohibited the taking of medicines prepared in advance. This was a rule which could be waived in the case of conditions which caused pain and discomfort: but if the principal prohibitions of plucking and grinding were involved, the treatment would be permitted on the Sabbath only if there was a danger to life. The next part of our text deals with such life-threatening conditions.

It is accepted in rabbinic literature that the duty of saving human life takes precedence over the rules against working on Shabbat: for example, if a pregnant woman goes into labour on Shabbat, it could be necessary to make all kinds of preparations otherwise prohibited: this was accepted and well-known.

The laws about the saving of animals on Shabbat are discussed above, at the end of the previous unit (p. 91).

Is it possible to tell whether or not there would have been more differences of opinion about these matters in the first century, before the Mishnah was redacted? Clearly, many of the categories listed in the Mishnah are by no means new. It is difficult to believe, for example, that there would have been different opinions in the first century about plucking corn on Shabbat – it was clearly prohibited. However, when considering the realm of medicine and what doctors were allowed to do, one is much closer to the frontiers of the *halakhah*, where there was room for dispute: some activities might be permitted, and others not. That doctors were available for consultation on Shabbat seems likely from Mishnah *Yoma* 8.5:

A sick person is fed at the word of experts.

Most modern scholars who have studied the mishnaic evidence are convinced that faith-healing without the use of medicines could not possibly infringe any of the Shabbat regulations.

Our text deals in some detail with the question of saving life on Shabbat. This particular halachic discussion is in the form of a *ma'aseh* – an actual event which took place. Because it involved well-known scholars, it was important for later generations to be aware of what they did and said. The names date the event to early in the second century. Notice how all of them were in agreement, without question, that the duty of saving life took precedence over the Sabbath – they only disputed what was the correct proof-text. Each of them gives a different answer to this. Rabbi Ishmael's was the first answer. He brings a proof-text from Exodus 22, which reads in full: 'If a thief be found in the very act of breaking in, and is struck so that he dies, there is no blood-guilt involved.' So in some circumstances, says scripture, it is permitted to kill a house-breaker: the background to this is that somebody who breaks in when the household is at home is considered to be potentially violent,[2] and so this was an act of self-defence. But if he is dead, you cannot cross-examine him, and Rabbi Ishmael points out that there may be some doubt as to whether he really came to steal or to kill, and he uses a *kal vahomer*, that is an *a fortiori* argument – if the shedding of blood overrides the Sabbath, how much more so does the saving of life? It is a very curious kind of argument: there may be certain circumstances in which one may have to kill somebody, even on Shabbat, even though killing somebody is such a serious matter: and if so, how much more so must Shabbat be broken to save life. The fact that Shabbat is not explicitly mentioned in the Exodus quotation does not matter: presumably the implication is that it is immaterial to Exodus whether the robber came on Friday night or any other night. So for the purposes of his argument, Rabbi Ishmael takes the case of his breaking in on Friday night.

Rabbi Elazar ben Azariah gives the next answer, and one much easier to understand. Circumcision of a new-born son takes places on the eighth day after the birth, and the Jewish tradition is that if the child was born on Shabbat, then the eighth day – counted inclusively – will also be Shabbat, and the circumcision takes place on that Shabbat. A whole chapter of Mishnah *Shabbat* is devoted to the question of which of the Sabbath restrictions can be broken on the occasion of a circumcision: carrying the instruments, putting on a bandage, and so on. Rabbi Elazar ben Azariah also uses a *kal vahomer* argument: he reasons that if circumcision which affects only one limb, takes precedence over Shabbat, how much more so must the whole body. If you can even break Shabbat for such a small physical matter, then for a really important physical matter, of course you can break Shabbat!

There is a very similar passage in John's Gospel about circumcision on Shabbat (John 7.22–23):

> Moses gave you circumcision (not that it is from Moses, but from the fathers) and you circumcise a man upon the sabbath. If on the sabbath a man receives circumcision, so that the law of Moses may not be broken, are you angry with me because on the sabbath I made a man's whole body well?

To return to the rabbinic text, to understand the next sentence it will be helpful to quote Lauterbach's translation, which is an expanded paraphrase: 'From the instance cited by you, it would also follow that just as there the Sabbath is to be disregarded only in a case of certainty, so here the Sabbath is to be disregarded only in a case of certainty'. This strange sentence states the argument used by the other rabbis to disagree with Rabbi Elazar ben Azariah's argument. For if there was some doubt as to whether the son was in fact born on Shabbat (for example, if the boy was born at twilight on Friday), then the circumcision would not be carried out on the next Shabbat, but be put off until the Saturday night or Sunday: only when it is certain that the boy was born on Shabbat is he to be circumcised on Shabbat. So the other rabbis object, that according to this argument, you could only break Shabbat to save a life when you are certain the person would otherwise die: but the *halakhah* is that you can break Shabbat in any case of *safek nefashot* – that is, a doubt about life. This phrase is particularly closely defined: certainly you can break Shabbat if it is certain somebody will die if you do not, but you can also break Shabbat within certain defined categories of doubt: some of the particular illnesses considered serious are discussed below.

Rabbi Akiva brings a different argument – from the Temple service. Some background knowledge is required here. We know that the Temple service involved 'work' on Shabbat, because it says explicitly in the Torah that various sacrifices had to be carried out on Shabbat, which involved killing the animal, tending the fires, roasting meat, and so on. So the Temple service overrides Shabbat. But murder overrides the Temple service: for it is stated (Ex. 21.14) that if a priest is about to sacrifice an animal in the Temple and somebody has come to the court accusing him of murder, then he can be dragged away from the sacrifice to be brought to trial for murder, even though that would interrupt the important task of performing sacrifices at the Temple: there is no sanctuary of the altar in Judaism. So a trial for murder supersedes the Temple service, and the Temple service supersedes Shabbat. Putting these together he comes to the conclusion that life-or-death matters supersede Shabbat.

The next opinion given is that of Rabbi Yossi the Galilean. His name was not actually mentioned as being present at this discussion, but his opinion was appended to our text. He brings the text our passage is actually discussing: 'My Sabbaths you shall keep', and he points out that this text actually begins with the Hebrew word *akh*, which means 'but' – 'But my Sabbaths you shall keep.' He sees the 'but' as a kind of limiting factor, some hint that keeping the Sabbath is to be limited in some way, and the exception, of course, is about saving life. He was following the precise method of derivation attributed to Rabbi Akiva and his followers.

Next is the opinion of Rabbi Shimon ben Menasia, who quotes the text 'It is holy to *you*', on which he comments that the Sabbath was handed to you, not you to the Sabbath – the famous and often quoted parallel to Jesus' statement (Mark 2.27): 'The sabbath was made for man, not man for the sabbath.' Both statements indicate that in certain circumstances human needs take precedence over the Shabbat laws: Shimon ben Menasia is clearly talking about the saving of life: the context of the statement in Mark is discussed below. Notice how the two statements are similar not only in content, but also in form (sabbath . . . man . . . man . . . sabbath – a chiasmus). Shimon lived in the mid second century CE. The closeness of his words to the Gospel saying makes it unlikely that the words were his own invention: probably both versions derive from the same oral tradition: both in Mark and in our text the saying gives the impression of being a common proverb which would carry more authority than the words of an individual speaker.

Finally, Rabbi Natan quotes 'keep the Sabbath to observe the Sabbath', which he interprets as one Sabbath leading to the next – and so if you save somebody's life, you may have broken one Sabbath, but the person whose life you have saved will be able to keep the next Sabbath.

Each rabbi thus brings a different text from the Bible to make his point. The argument is not just academic, but the proof chosen could affect practical details of the law: thus Elazar ben Azariah's argument is rejected as covering only certainty that somebody might die, not a case of doubt.

The next text gives an example of what was considered a danger to life. It mentions a sore throat, which we might today not think of as particularly serious:

31 *Mishnah, Yoma 8.6*

If somebody is seized with a manic hunger, they may feed him even unclean things until his eyes light up. If a mad dog bit him, they must not feed him the lobe of its liver, but Rabbi Matya ben Heresh permits it. And Rabbi Matya ben Heresh also said, If somebody has a sore throat, they may drop medicine into his mouth on the Sabbath, because there is a doubt about his life, and danger to life overrides the Sabbath.

This gives some indication of the kind of illness which might have been considered serious. It did not have to be what we would call a fatal disease – in ancient times very many more ailments were potentially dangerous than is the case today. Similarly, in the Catholic tradition baptism is normally performed by a priest, but in danger of death anyone may baptize – and this does not mean just a definite danger, but a doubt. In both cases the idea is to err on the side of safety.

It seems clear, however, that in mishnaic times an illness or injury was not generally considered a danger to life unless it was one which affected the whole body, or an organ the loss of which could be a danger, such as the eyes. It is stated elsewhere (Mishnah *Shabbat* 22.6) that it was not permitted to set a broken limb on the Sabbath: no harm, it was thought, would be caused by waiting.

Setting a broken limb was considered to come under the category of 'building'. It should be pointed out that the rabbis of the Talmud rejected this particular ruling, and permitted setting a fracture on Shabbat (Talmud *Shabbat* 148 A).

The first part of our text deals with cases where it might be necessary to break the dietary laws for the saving of life, and the second part with cases where it might be necessary to break Shabbat. In both cases the principle is the same, that doubt about life supersedes these laws. In fact the saving of life overrides all laws except the prohibitions on murder, prohibited sexual relations (such as incest, rape and adultery), and idolatry.

Our first Gospel texts deal with the question of the disciples who plucked corn on the Sabbath. In all three Synoptic Gospels, the stories quoted are followed immediately by accounts of Jesus' healing on the Sabbath: there is a clear intention to multiply examples, just as the rabbinic texts do.

When reading the following texts, it is important to notice the reference to David and to look up the story in I Samuel, chapter 21, verses 1–6: David there is a fugitive, being pursued by Saul, and takes the bread of the Presence from Ahimelech the priest, who keeps the Ark of the covenant. There does seem to be some strong need for the bread, which overrides the normal procedures in the shrine. But is there any parallel between the need of the disciples and the need of David and his men when they were on the run?

Matthew 12.1–8

32

[1]At that time Jesus went through the grainfields on the sabbath; his disciples were hungry, and they began to pluck ears of grain and to eat. [2]But when the Pharisees saw it, they said to him, 'Look, your disciples are doing what is not lawful to do on the sabbath.' [3]He said to them, 'Have you not read what David did, when he was hungry, and those who were with him: [4]how he entered the house of God and ate the bread of the Presence, which it was not lawful for him to eat nor for those who were with him, but only for the priests? [5]Or have you not read in the law how on the sabbath the priests in the temple profane the sabbath, and are guiltless? [6]I tell you, something greater than the temple is here. [7]And if you had known what this means, "I desire mercy, and not sacrifice," you would not have condemned the guiltless. [8]For the Son of man is lord of the sabbath.'

(ii) Mark 2.23–28

[23]One sabbath he was going through the grainfields: and as they made

their way his disciples began to pluck ears of grain. [24]And the Pharisees said to him, 'Look, why are they doing what is not lawful on the sabbath?' [25]And he said to them, 'Have you never read what David did, when he was in need and was hungry, he and those who were with him: [26]how he entered the house of God, when Abiathar was high priest, and ate the bread of the Presence, which it is not lawful for any but the priest to eat, and also gave it to those who were with him?' [27]And he said to them, 'The sabbath was made for man, not man for the sabbath; [28]so the Son of man is lord even of the sabbath.'

(iii) Luke 6.1–5

[1]On a sabbath, while he was going through the grainfields, his disciples plucked and ate some ears of grain, rubbing them in their hands. [2]But some of the Pharisees said, 'Why are you doing what is not lawful to do on the sabbath?' [3]And Jesus answered, 'Have you not read what David did when he was hungry, he and those who were with him: [4]how he entered the house of God, and took and ate the bread of the Presence, which it is not lawful for any but the priests to eat, and also gave it to those with him?' [5]And he said to them, 'The Son of man is lord of the sabbath.'

Notice that this passage is not a debate about Jesus himself breaking the Sabbath, but about an action carried out by the disciples who were with him. Jesus could not be held responsible for what they did, but seems willing to debate the issue. The disciples pluck and eat grain on the Sabbath. Now we know the plucking of corn was prohibited on the Sabbath: Luke, as if to emphasize this point, adds the *melakhah* of grinding ('rubbing them in their hands'). Why then did they break Shabbat? The only clue given is in Matthew's narrative, where it states that they were hungry (verse 1). One theory is that it was an emergency: they were fleeing from Herod or from the Romans, and in danger of their lives. There is, however, no indication of this in the text: on the contrary, the incident is related as a chance event ('one sabbath' in Mark), and it is difficult to imagine that individual grains would make much of a meal.

How are we to understand Jesus' reply to the accusations made by the Pharisees? Is he taking part in a halachic debate? Is he objecting to the law itself, or suggesting that it does not apply to his disciples? Is he seeking to change the law? Certainly his reply in Matthew shows some knowledge of the issues debated by the rabbis. This is clear from Matthew 12.5, where Jesus describes how the Torah states that the priests in the Temple profane the Sabbath. In fact this is nowhere stated in the written Torah: the statement implies a knowledge of the traditional list of prohibited tasks, which included the slaughtering of animals. Jesus' statement about the Temple services is repeated frequently in the Talmud (e.g. *Yevamot* 32B), and is used by Rabbi Akiva in the text from the *Mekhilta* discussed above. There is thus strong evidence here that the 'law' of Judaism in Matthew's time was the 'law' of the rabbis, and that we are justified in comparing rabbinic texts written down much later.

Jesus begins his response, however, by making a different point, comparing himself and his disciples to David and his followers. However, the incident with David had nothing to do with Shabbat. How then is it a reply to the accusation of breaking Shabbat? One link is that David took the food both for himself and those with him, and it was Jesus' disciples who took the grain. But there is undoubtedly more to Jesus' use of the story of David than this. Mark and Luke present only this line of reasoning: there was an urgency for David and his followers to eat whatever was available: David was able to break the law. But in Matthew's narrative, it makes sense to link the words about David with what follows. Jesus' argument seems to run like this: you know that the service in the Temple overrides the Sabbath: you know that David and his companions set aside the service in the sanctuary because they were hungry: therefore David, or somebody else who could be regarded as a king, can override the Sabbath. This interpretation would fit well with the final line that the Son of Man has authority over the Sabbath, assuming that Jesus is referring to himself by the phrase 'Son of man'. Matthew's argument effectively has three parts: there is something greater than David here: there is something greater than the Temple here (verse 6): and there is something greater than the Sabbath here. The whole tone of the narratives does not give the impression that this was one of those occasions when breaking the Sabbath would have been allowed, but rather that the 'lord of the sabbath' can do as he wishes.

Notice how Jesus' logic differs from that used by Rabbi Akiva. In the *Mekhilta* passage, the argument is used to justify a ruling they were already sure about: they all knew that the saving of life overrides the Sabbath, but they wanted to back up their belief with a scriptural proof. Jesus' argument differs, in that he seems to be using scripture to say something entirely new. The method is rabbinic, but the use to which it is put is totally different.

Notice what happens in verses 27–28 in Mark and in verse 8 in Matthew: both of them clinch the discussion by the point that the Son of man is Lord even of the Sabbath, but only Mark precedes it by the statement: 'The sabbath was made for man, not man for the sabbath.' It is as if Matthew has deliberately edited out the phrase which is known to be related to a rabbinic discussion – as if he were stating that he knew there were circumstances in which breaking Shabbat could be justified, but this story is about something rather different – 'the Son of man is lord of the sabbath'. The phrase 'lord of the sabbath' is itself a strange one: it is a very strong claim to make, as the Sabbath has just been described as God's gift to man. The Greek word *kurios* means literally 'having power or authority over', suggesting perhaps a person entitled to legislate for others about how to keep the Sabbath – but the word is also used in the Septuagint to mean 'God' – so perhaps here also it is suggesting that the Son of man has a share in the divine essence.

This interpretation raises another question: could a Jew of Jesus' time break the law in this way? Is his a sufficient argument for doing something which is otherwise not allowed? If God's Law has really prohibited something, who is in a position to say – don't listen to that? This was not one of those occasions when it could have been allowed: the Gospel story is presented clearly saying: this is not one of those occasions, but he still sanctioned it.

The text can be read in a different way if we question the assumption that Jesus was referring to himself in the phrase 'Son of man'. The Hebrew equivalent, *ben Adam*, means simply 'a man': However, in the Book of Ezekiel, the phrase 'Son of man' is frequently used by God in addressing the prophet. There is a huge scholarly literature on this subject, which is clearly summarized in *Jesus the Jew* by Geza Vermes.[3] The meaning of the phrase will long be disputed: for our purposes it is worth pointing out that if the phrase is a periphrasis for 'man', then 'The Son of man is lord of the sabbath' may be little different from the rabbinic saying, 'The sabbath was handed to you, not you to the Sabbath.'

Thus Jews and Christians ask different questions and have different reactions to this text. Jews will ask 'What was Jesus teaching?' 'What did he really mean?' Christians ask 'Who *was* this man who could break God's Law?' 'Who really was he?' Just as the rabbis could use quotation and argument to justify or support a conclusion they already knew, so here the telling of the story seems designed to support the conclusion about the 'Son of man'. The concern of the evangelists was not the concern of *halakhah*.

Jesus does not seem to be stating that the law in itself is wrong, or should be changed, but rather that his disciples can be exempted from this restriction. The narrative begins like a rabbinic story, but swiftly moves outside the concerns of the rabbis into matters of interest to the early Christian community.

Our next texts are a selection of the stories about Jesus healing on the Sabbath. The first three parallel texts are direct continuations of the texts about plucking grain: three other texts follow.

33

(i) Matthew 12.9–14

[9]And he went on from there, and entered their synagogue. [10]And behold, there was a man with a withered hand. And they asked him, 'Is it lawful to heal on the sabbath?' so that they might accuse him. [11]He said to them, 'What man of you, if he has one sheep and it falls into a pit on the sabbath, will not lay hold of it and lift it out? [12]Of how much more value is a man than a sheep! So it is lawful to do good on the sabbath.' [13]Then he said to the man, 'Stretch out your hand.' And the man stretched it out, and it was restored, whole like the other. [14]But the Pharisees went out and took counsel against him, how to destroy him.

(ii) Mark 3.1–6

[1]Again he entered the synagogue, and a man was there who had a withered hand. [2]And they watched him, to see whether he would heal him on the sabbath, so that they might accuse him. [3]And he said to the man who had the withered hand, 'Come here.' [4]And he said to them, 'Is it lawful on the sabbath to do good or do harm, to save life or to kill?' But they were silent. [5]And he looked around at them with anger, grieved at their hardness of heart, and said to the man, 'Stretch out your hand.' He stretched it out, and his hand was restored. [6]The Pharisees went out, and immediately held counsel with the Herodians against him, how to destroy him.

(iii) Luke 6.6–11

[6]On another sabbath, when he entered the synagogue and taught, a man was there whose right hand was withered. [7]And the scribes and the Pharisees watched him, to see whether he would heal on the sabbath, so that they might find an accusation against him. [8]But he knew their thoughts, and he said to the man who had the withered hand, 'Come and stand here.' And he rose and stood there. [9]And Jesus said to them, 'I ask you, is it lawful on the sabbath to do good or to do harm, to save life or to destroy it?' [10]And he looked around on them all, and said to him, 'Stretch out your hand.' And he did so, and his hand was restored. [11]But they

were filled with fury and discussed with one another what they might do to Jesus.

34   Luke 13.10–17

[10]Now he was teaching in one of the synagogues on the sabbath. [11]And there was a woman who had had a spirit of infirmity for eighteen years; she was bent over and could not fully straighten herself. [12]And when Jesus saw her, he called her and said to her, 'Woman, you are freed from your infirmity.' [13]And he laid his hands upon her, and immediately she was made straight, and she praised God. [14]But the ruler of the synagogue, indignant because Jesus had healed on the sabbath, said to the people, 'There are six days on which work ought to be done: come on those days, and be healed, and not on the sabbath day.' [15]Then the Lord answered him, 'You hypocrites! Does not each of you on the sabbath untie his ox or his ass from the manger, and lead it away to water it? [16]And ought not this woman, a daughter of Abraham whom Satan bound for eighteen years, be loosed from this bond on the sabbath day?' [17]As he said this, all his adversaries were put to shame; and all the people rejoiced at all the glorious things that were done by him.

35   Luke 14.1–6

[1]One sabbath when he went to dine at the house of a ruler who belonged to the Pharisees, they were watching him. [2]And behold, there was a man before him who had dropsy. [3]And Jesus spoke to the lawyers and Pharisees, saying, 'Is it lawful to heal on the sabbath, or not?' [4]But they were silent. Then he took him and healed him, and let him go. [5]And he said to them, 'Which of you, having an ass or an ox that has fallen into a well, will not immediately pull him out on a sabbath day?' [6]And they could not reply to this.

36   John 5.1–18

[1]After this there was a feast of the Jews, and Jesus went up to Jerusalem.
[2]Now there is in Jerusalem by the Sheep Gate a pool, in Hebrew called Beth-zatha, which has five porticoes. [3]In these lay a multitude of invalids, blind, lame, paralysed. [5]One man was there, who had been ill for thirty-eight years. [6]When Jesus saw him and knew that he had been lying there a long time, he said to him, 'Do you want to be healed?' [7]The sick man answered him, 'Sir, I have no man to put me into the pool when the water is troubled, and while I am going another steps down before me.' [8]Jesus said to him, 'Rise, take up your pallet, and walk.' [9]And at once the man was healed, and he took up his pallet and walked.

Now that day was the sabbath. [10]So the Jews said to the man who was cured, 'It is the sabbath, it is not lawful for you to carry your pallet.' [11]But he answered them, 'The man who healed me said to me, "Take up your pallet, and walk."' [12]They asked him, 'Who is the man who said to you, "Take up your pallet, and walk"?' [13]Now the man who had been healed did not know who it was, for Jesus had withdrawn, as there was a crowd in the place. [14]Afterward, Jesus found him in the temple, and said to him, 'See, you are well! Sin no more, that nothing worse befall you.' [15]The man went away and told the Jews that it was Jesus who had healed him. [16]And this was why the Jews persecuted Jesus, because he did this on the sabbath. [17]But Jesus answered them, 'My Father is working still, and I am working.' [18]This was why the Jews sought all the more to kill him, because he not only broke the sabbath but also called God his Father, making himself equal with God.

In these texts, is there anything Jesus is doing here to break the Sabbath according to the mishnaic definition? In the first story he tells the man to stretch out his hand: in text 35 all he does is speak, and in text 34 he lays on hands. In John (text 36) he does no work himself, but he makes the man carry his bed. It will be recalled that 'work' on the Sabbath consisted of carrying out specific acts of *melakhah*. Preparing medicines was prohibited, but Jesus uses no medicines. He does not appear to be doing anything which the rabbis would have called 'profaning the Sabbath'. It may be that there were other popular ideas about Sabbath 'work' not recorded in the rabbinic sources: perhaps if Jesus was regarded as some kind of professional healer, it might be thought he should have had a day off: 'there are six days on which work ought to be done' (Luke 13.14) – the ruler of the synagogue was indignant – he does not say he was wrong.

Certainly, in these texts also, there are elements of halachic debate. In text 33 (i), Jesus talks about rescuing an animal from a pit on the Sabbath, an act prohibited according to rabbinic sources. In text 33, versions (ii) and (iii), Jesus uses the argument that it is correct to save life on the Sabbath. In text 34 Jesus suggests that the 'hypocrites' break the Sabbath by untying an animal, an act clearly prohibited. In text 35, the Pharisees seem unable to deny that healing on the Sabbath is permitted. In text 36 it is pointed out that it was prohibited on the Sabbath to carry in a public place. So all the evangelists seem to have some knowledge of the rabbinic *halakhah*. All the more strange then, that the arguments should be centred around the notion of healing, an activity apparently not prohibited.

It is important to point out, however, that many aspects of rabbinic halakhah were not finally fixed at this time, but open to debate. Another way of reading these debates is that Jesus is not so much taunting the Pharisees for their own non-observance of the law, but presenting his own opinion on the issues – that in his view it is permitted on Shabbat to take an animal from a pit, or to untie one in order to feed it. It is correct to do good and to save life, and thus correct also to heal.

Yet another way of looking at these debates is to think of Shabbat not in terms of the rabbinic definitions of work, but in terms of the account in Genesis 1–2, where God completes the work of creation and rests on the seventh day. God in a sense created by speaking ('And God said: Let there be light') – and Jesus seems to heal by speaking. Healing in these texts was perhaps regarded as a kind of completion of God's creation – hence in John Jesus says 'My Father is working still, and I am working' – real rest cannot come until creation is complete. In text 32 above, Mark 2.27, Jesus states that the sabbath was *made* for man, whereas the rabbinic parallel is that the 'Sabbath is *given*' – the first statement focusses more on the creation story, the second on the covenant at Sinai where God gave the laws. In the narratives about healing, there is perhaps an idea that as Shabbat is a holy day, it was therefore easier to heal then. Healing came from God, and so the fact this was done on the day dedicated to his service may be significant. However, in many of the stories, Jesus uses the argument that other people are breaking Shabbat also – as if healing was normally prohibited on that day. For example, there is the argument in Luke, text 34, about the ox and ass: it would have been acceptable to give them water on Shabbat, but not to untie them: in the same way, says Jesus, the woman is 'loosed' from her bond. In this passage Jesus came to be criticizing those who were not scrupulous about their observance of Shabbat.

Is it significant that some of the stories are of healing inside the synagogue? It was a meeting place, especially on the Sabbath, and no doubt all kinds of activities took place there. Notice that at this time (Luke, text 34) there was no separation between the men and the women in this synagogue: an example of how a Gospel text can enhance our understanding of Jewish history. It is interesting to note also in this passage that the objection came from the ruler of the synagogue, not from a rabbi or Pharisee. The reference seems to be to the official known in rabbinic literature as a *hazzan*, whose task it was to bring out the scrolls, to open them to the readings, and put them away (Mishnah *Yoma* 7.1). Perhaps the text is not making a halachic point at all. Did being in the synagogue make a difference? In Mark 1.21–28 (cf. Luke 4.31ff.) a scene is recounted in which Jesus expels an unclean spirit from a man in the synagogue on Shabbat. But there was no protest whatsoever, which seems to heighten the idea that there is something deliberately being provoked in the way our texts are narrated. The first story seems to be told because the evangelist is concerned about the clash between Jesus and the evil spirit. Our narratives seem to be told to make a point about Shabbat, and about clashes with the Jewish authorities.

If, however, one puts aside the rabbinic evidence, the clear implication of the Gospel narratives as they have come down to us is that Jesus *was* breaking the Sabbath by healing: 'And the scribes and the Pharisees watched him, to see whether he would heal on the sabbath, so that they might find an accusation against him.' Some have linked this to debates in the church about whether Christians should continue to keep Shabbat: they needed to have precedents that Jesus declared it to be abrogated. The portrayal of the Pharisees in many of these narratives gives a sense of a caricature without substance – stock characters using stock arguments, without any of the liveliness of debate found in the mishnaic passages. Neither the characters nor their arguments were of real interest to the evangelists.

The narrative in John (text 36) has rather a different tone from the others. The pool of Beth-zatha was by the side of the Temple in Jerusalem. Only half way through the story is it mentioned that it was the Sabbath: the first 9 verses, taken alone, have a very different tone from what follows. In the second half of the story, the 'Jews' seem to nurture a personal hatred for Jesus himself: they consider him to hold blasphemous ideas. Some details of John's narrative are puzzling. What did Jesus mean, for example, when he asks the man to 'Sin no more'? Is it an allusion to his having been told off for carrying his pallet? It does not seem to be a reference to his illness. And at first it seems that the objection of the Jews was not to Jesus' healing but telling the man to carry his pallet – clearly prohibited in a public place on Shabbat. Only in verse 16 is the objection to his healing appended. And why did Jesus make this man do something which was going to be so provocative to the community? At that moment, he was so awe-struck that he would have done anything he was told to. And what is the implication of his failing to know that it was Jesus who had healed him? Was this his 'sin'?

Some of the difficulties in this narrative may be solved by comparing a similar story in Mark 2.1–12. In this story the invalid is let down before Jesus on his pallet through a hole in the roof. There is no suggestion that this was Shabbat. The phrase 'take up your pallet and go home' is coupled by Jesus with the preamble 'that you may know that the Son of man has authority on earth to forgive sins'. Perhaps John, aware of this other story, associated in his mind the spiritual and the physical healing.

Perhaps the evangelists brought the stories to emphasize that Jesus was in fact in conflict with the authorities over certain aspects of the Sabbath, in order to justify their own failure to keep the Sabbath customs. This would be similar to the process we have seen in the rabbinic texts – trying to link an existing situation to a justification from history. In similar fashion, thirty years earlier, the Council of Jerusalem tried to justify the ruling that gentile converts to Christianity did not have to be circumcised. There is also an additional significance to the phrase 'Lord of the Sabbath', for this is what they believed Jesus to be. John's text ends with a clear reference to the divinity of Jesus. This is a subject logically connected with the Sabbath debates. Who created the Sabbath and is Lord of it? He who made it has power to overrule it. A close analysis of these Gospel narratives indicates a clear departure by the evangelists from Jewish tradition, not only in attitudes to the Sabbath, but in the new theology of the nature of Christ.

Points for Discussion: Models for Dialogue

In recent years, it has become common for Christians to seek guidance from Jews about the Jewish background to the Gospels, and many Jewish scholars have been happy to help in this enterprise. The 'Sabbath' stories have been discussed, argued over and analysed in very many books, articles, lectures and seminars. It is worth reflecting that such enterprises reflect a certain presupposition about the nature of the relationship between the two faiths, which is shared by many Jews and Christians today. We often continue our dialogue without precisely understanding this, and realizing what our assumptions are.

Often, when Christians come to Jews to discover their 'authentic roots', they assume the existence of a Hebrew tradition, which has had a linear development right through to contemporary

Judaism: somewhere along the route there was an offshoot which we know as Christianity. The unspoken model for such dialogue looks something like this:

The traditional Christian outlook is very different from this. The Church Fathers, like many theologians right up to the present day, regarded the Hebrew tradition as showing a linear development to Christianity, from which, at a particular period of time, the Jewish people somehow became diverted. This model of the development of the two faiths looks something like this:

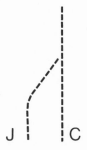

This model sees the church as the true Israel, from which rabbinic Judaism departed because it would not accept Jesus who was the true continuation of the Hebrew tradition. Obviously, the model we adopt for dialogue will make a tremendous difference on such issues as how we view the possession of the Hebrew scriptures; and where we look for a true interpretation of the Hebrew scriptures on such matters as how to celebrate the Sabbath.

These two models are mirror images of each other. The reader may like to ponder, in the light of the texts studied, whether it is not now possible to create a new model for dialogue:

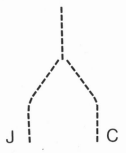

In this model, as in the others, the Hebrew tradition developed up to a particular time of division. It suggests, however, that Judaism (as it develops through the rabbis and continues) and Christianity (as interpreted through the Gospels) can both be seen as equally authentic interpretations and developments of that one common Hebrew tradition and scripture. In other words, the parent-child image of dialogue is not necessarily the best image, but another model is possible, in which we see ourselves as twins from the same parent.

This proposed new model makes a difference to the way the Hebrew scriptures are to be regarded in dialogue. In the first model, which today many modern Christians follow, the scriptures are very clearly the Jewish scriptures from which Christianity has branched off. One modern Christian theologian has stated that any Christians reading the Hebrew Bible are eavesdropping on somebody else's private conversation with God. The second model, on the other hand, reflects the old Christian theological presupposition that the New Testament and Christian theology give the only really true understanding of the Hebrew Bible, and the Jewish tradition does not understand its inheritance.

Can we doubt that it is a blessing today that we have a common heritage in the Hebrew scriptures? Jews would not have been readmitted into Britain under Cromwell had it not been for that common heritage. One important element in dialogue is to recognize a joint heritage, and recognize that we may interpret texts in different ways without calling our own tradition the only valid interpretation.

On the other hand, one might well argue that the Hebrew Bible in the original language has over the centuries been the heritage of the Jews: the fact is that the Hebrew scriptures were preserved in Hebrew by them, and not by Christians. Because for many years the Western churches were using translations, (the Eastern church also used a translation, but a Jewish one, the Septuagint), and the translation became the text, there was inevitably a departure from the original. It is only in more recent times that the common heritage of the Hebrew Bible has become more of a blessing than a stumbling block to dialogue.

In considering our own selected time of study, the first century CE, it is important to be aware of the Jewish tradition that it was at Yavneh, after the destruction, that the canon of the Hebrew Bible was finally settled.[4] The Christians too were engaged in the same process at this time. Because Temple worship was gone, there was felt a need to reflect on what remained.

The new model presupposes that Jews and Christians began to develop different customs and beliefs in contradistinction to each other. Certainly in medieval times we know this was true: this may well be the origin of Jewish men covering their heads for prayer, for example. Many other practices may well have developed out of the rift between the two faiths. The question which this work discusses is whether this process of polemic was actually taking place in the very early days of Christianity: this is much more difficult to answer, because it appears at first sight that we only possess one side of the debate. In the Christian scriptures, there are very many references to Jews; in the rabbinic writings as they have survived there are very few references to Christians. One reason for this could be that the early Christians were seen as a small fringe group who went their own way, whom it was not worth taking any notice of: this answer would make the first model the correct one for analysing texts from our period: another reason is that during the Middle Ages much Jewish literature was actually censored by Christians, and it was not possible for literature which contained anti-Christian remarks to survive. To this day, the text of the Talmud, when discussing non-Jews and apostates, uses a huge variety of words: *min, goy, epikoros, nokhri* and so on: often one can find one copy of a book which has one text, and another which has another one of these terms: the words had become censored, and it is impossible to work out what the text originally said. So half the debate is actually missing, and we are trying in modern times to reconstruct what was going on. Can we work out whether or not rabbinic Judaism was influenced by a reaction against early Christian practice?

The modern attempt to reconstruct the early debates has to avoid the problems caused by our medieval heritage, when the whole point of reading somebody else's writings was to prove them wrong. The passages they selected and quoted were always those which could be read in the worst possible light. This happened on both sides. Two of the most frequently quoted writers in Thomas Aquinas are Maimonides and Avicenna – they are quoted in his objections to give him a platform for what he wants to say in retaliation. They were read very critically.

The idea that there is anything of value to be gained by looking at each other's texts constructively is comparatively new. We are in the infancy of dialogue, laying the foundations for future generations: even the collections of parallel texts which have been prepared before, by Strack-Billerbeck and others, have had two major faults. First, they attempt to find parallel texts from any source, whether typical of rabbinic thinking or not: and secondly, there has also been a tendency to find passages which show one side as being better than the other.

The reader may wish to reflect on the difference each of the three models would make to the way one views the texts on the Sabbath. With the first model as a guide, we would view Jesus as portrayed in the Gospels making a clear break with Jewish tradition: with the second model as a guide, we would view the Gospel texts as portraying the real meaning of a Sabbath of compassion and healing. If we adopt the third model, can we regard the year 70 as the turning point, when Judaism and Christianity began to oppose each other? And can we not find elements caused by bitter polemic, as well as a great deal of value, in both traditions?

Unit Six

Divorce

Initial point of comparison:
Halachic

The aim of this unit is to compare and contrast the Gospel and rabbinic teachings on divorce.

Divorce law is an issue which causes contemporary problems and heartbreak in the Jewish world, in the Christian world, and in society at large. The issues within each community are different. While discussion among Christians has focussed on the issue of whether divorce should be permitted, in Jewish communities the main issue has been the right of a woman to initiate divorce proceedings. This unit looks at some of the principal primary sources from both traditions, sources which reveal the issues in ancient times, as well as shedding light on the debates of our own time.

The Torah permits divorce. The relevant scriptural text is Deuteronomy 24.1, which reads:

> If a man takes a wife and marries her, and it comes to pass that she finds no favour in his eyes because he has found some indecency in her, then he shall write her a document of divorce, and put it into her hand, and send her out of his house.

Most translations make this verse only part of a sentence, but from the Hebrew it is clear that the verse can stand alone.

The word translated 'indecency' (many translations give 'some unseemly thing') is in Hebrew *ervat davar*. Now *Erva* has the root meaning of 'nakedness', and has the specific legal meaning of an unpermitted sexual union: the prohibited relationships are listed in Leviticus 18 and 20: 'You shall not uncover the nakedness of your father's wife' etc. The word there for 'nakedness' is also *erva*, which has the more general sense of adultery or incest or rape or any other prohibited sexual union. Note, however, that our passage begins with another phrase – 'if she finds no favour in his eyes'. From our text we cannot tell if this is an *alternative* reason for divorce or an *additional* reason for divorce: does it mean *either* she has done something wrong *or* she finds no favour in his eyes, or does it mean *both* she has committed adultery or incest *and* she finds no favour in his eyes? From the biblical text it is impossible to tell.

Notice from the text that the divorce document must be written: there are other references in the Torah to writing, but not very many. Most scholars date Deuteronomy from the seventh century BCE, the time of King Josiah: so at this period there must have been a written divorce document in use: our verse calls it a *sefer keritut*, literally 'a book of cutting': but in rabbinic literature a divorce document is called a *get*, and there were very elaborate rules about how to write it and what it had to say. These rules form the subject of a tractate of the Mishnah and Talmud, entitled *Gittin* (the plural of *get*). In our period, if a *get* was worded or delivered incorrectly, it was not valid, and this meant that any subsequent remarriage by the woman would also be considered invalid, and would have the status of an adulterous union. The man, however, was in theory permitted to have a second wife, as Jacob did, although one wife was the norm: there is not a single case of bigamy among the thousands of stories about the Rabbis in the Mishnah and Talmud.[1] So for a husband to remarry without correctly divorcing his first wife is not prohibited in biblical law.

Adultery in Jewish law is defined as follows: if a married woman has intercourse with a man who is not her husband, both parties commit adultery. If a married man has intercourse with a single woman, this is not technically adultery, since he is in theory allowed more than one wife. In ancient times, adultery carried the death penalty, but there had to be witnesses to the act. Adultery must be clearly distinguished from sexual relations between unmarried couples: although the rabbis prohibited this, it was not considered to be a prohibition from the *Torah*: it was an offence far less serious than adultery.

The second part of the divorce process is that, as the text says, the man has to put the divorce document into her hand: rabbinic law interpreted this as meaning that the *get* has to be given or delivered by the husband to his wife, and she has to accept the delivery. If the document is not delivered or not accepted, then the marriage is still in operation. Thus the writing of the *get* and its delivery are the two main parts of the divorce, and either of these can be performed by an agent, as can many other *mitzvot*.

There is no biblical reference to any written document for marriage itself, only for divorce. It does seem that in early biblical times there may well have been no marriage ceremony at all, the woman simply coming into the man's tent or house. However, in the post-biblical period, it is likely that there were also documents for marriage: and in rabbinic Judaism there was certainly a marriage document or contract, known as a *ketubah*. The importance of this document is connected with divorce: because the main provision of the *ketubah* is an agreement that if the marriage is dissolved (a marriage can only end in two ways, by divorce or death) then a sum of money is given by the husband to the wife for her future maintenance. The amount was laid down in writing as a provision of the contract, and was witnessed to that effect. As we shall see, the financial provisions of the *ketubah* are certainly ancient, and no doubt were originally designed to prevent divorced women or widows living in poverty. The document still remains an essential part of Jewish marriage, although the financial provisions now have a symbolic rather than a practical value.

There are also other documents mentioned in ancient sources: for example, there may well have been a betrothal document, but it is these two, the *ketubah* and the *get*, which are the main ones, and the two with which we are familiar today.

To return to Deuteronomy 24, it is important to realize that there is a second example of case law there (Deut. 24.1–4):

> If a man takes a wife and marries her, and it comes to pass that she finds no favour in his eyes because he has found some indecency in her, then he shall write her a document of divorce, and put it into her hand, and send her out of his house: and she will go out of his house, and may go and be another man's wife: but if the second husband hates her, and writes her a document of divorce, and puts it in her hand and sends her from his house – or if the second husband dies, who took her to be his wife – then her first husband, who sent her away, may not again take her to be his wife, after she has been made impure: for that is an abomination to the Lord.

This was interpreted by the rabbis as a separate and second case, which prevents a woman remarrying her husband if she has been married to somebody else in the interim.

When we turn to the rabbinic texts, it will be noticed that the first concern of the rabbis was to protect the rights of the woman through the provisions of the *ketubah*:

Tosefta Ketubot 12.1   **37**

Originally, when her marriage settlement (*ketubah*) was kept by her father, it seemed an easy thing to him to divorce her, so Shimon ben Shetah legislated that the marriage settlement should be kept by her husband, and he wrote for her that 'All the property which will come to me is held liable and on pledge to pay you your marriage settlement.'

The word *ketubah* is used both for the marriage contract as a whole, and for the sum of money stipulated in it, which the husband has to pay to his wife in the event of divorce.

Shimon ben Shetah lived at the end of the second century BCE, long before the time of the Gospels: this, then, was one of the earliest post-biblical reforms of Jewish law. The first word, 'Originally', clearly refers to the time *before* Shimon ben Shetah, sometime in the second century. At this time, we can deduce from our text, the money for the *ketubah* was set aside at the time of marriage and kept for her by her father in safety, to ensure that it was immediately available for her in the event of divorce. This rule was clearly designed for a poor woman's protection in an era when she would have been unlikely to have her own property – but the rule clearly created a difficulty: as the money was set aside at marriage, it made marriage expensive and divorce easy. The husband did not have to find the money on divorce, but simply to write and deliver a *get*, and send his wife to her father's house for her maintenance. In the later discussion of this text, the Talmud suggests that because of the old rule women were reluctant to marry – the men grew old and could not find a wife. Perhaps men also may have been reluctant to marry, because they had to find the whole sum of money in advance. So Shimon ben Shetah decreed that in future the husband could marry without finding the sum of money in advance: he had to find it only if he wanted a divorce: in order to protect the wife and make sure she received the money, the whole of his property could if necessary be sequestered by the court for it. This is still the practice today. Although property generally remained in the control of men in a male dominated society, the situation described at least provided some protection for the woman.

It will be understood from this legislation that marriage in Judaism is a contract which contains within its provisions the procedure for its dissolution. The text shows that the *ketubah* is at least as old as the second century BCE, and so would certainly have been in use in the time of Jesus. Many of the most important provisions for divorce can be found in the tractate *Ketubot* (= marriage contracts, the plural of *ketubah*). The next text is taken from there:

38 *Mishnah Ketubot 7.6*

The following are divorced without their marriage settlement: she who transgresses Mosaic or Jewish law. And what is meant here by Mosaic law? If she fed him food which had not been tithed, or slept with him during her period, or did not separate the dough, or made a vow and did not keep it. And what is meant here by Jewish law? If she goes out with her hair loose, or spins in the market-place, or speaks with all men. Abba Saul said, Also if she curses his parents before him. Rabbi Tarfon says, Also if she is loud-mouthed. What is meant here by loud mouthed? One who speaks in her house so that her neighbours can hear her voice.

This text, which clearly reveals the male prejudices of its author, contains a list of misdemeanours which a divorced wife might possibly have committed. It is important to understand that the misdemeanours quoted are not *grounds* for divorce: the halachic point is that in such cases the husband is allowed, *if* he divorces her, to take away her right to the *ketubah*, the money stipulated for the marriage settlement to which she would otherwise be entitled.

One fascinating aspect of this text is the distinction it appears to make between 'Mosaic' and 'Jewish' law. The *dat Moshe* clearly refers to matters of *halakhah* – prohibited by the Torah. The *dat yehudit* are not matters which come under such a clearly defined legal category: but rather things which depart from a cultural norm of the kind of way women were expected to behave in that particular society. The first part, the *dat Moshe*, could be regarded as universally applicable from generation to generation: the *dat yehudit* depends on the custom of the time and place of the Mishnah. It is in fact unusual for the Mishnah to use the term 'Jewish': it was a term which seems to have been used mainly by other people writing about Jews: the term occurs in the Book of Esther, and was the normal term used by the Romans and in the Gospels. The normal rabbinic term, however, for a Jew is *Yisrael*. In our text it does seem that the word 'Jewish' is being used in a sense of 'ethnic and cultural identity', whereas *dat Moshe* carries a sense of *halakhah*. This implies that the word 'Jew' could bear a sense different from *Yisrael*. A *Yisrael* is somebody who follows the religion of Moses: a Jew is somebody who is part of a social group, who follows the customs of that people. This distinction may help in understanding the many references to Jews in John's Gospel. Where Jesus is disputing on matters of law, his adversaries are not often called Jews – but Pharisees or rabbis: but where the evangelist writes about a crowd or a group of people who are not necessarily lawyers, the term 'Jew' is used.

The statement of the second-century rabbi Abba Saul fits better with the 'Mosaic' than the 'Jewish' law. It should perhaps be read as a comment appended to the whole paragraph, not just to the immediately preceding part.

From this text one can see an example of how the tractate *Ketubot* goes into some detail about the kind of circumstances in which people might get divorced: the tractate *Gittin* (divorce documents) deals almost entirely with the divorce document itself, and how to write it, and what it should say, the kind of ink and paper, and whether you are allowed to throw it away, and many other such details. It is only at the very end that there is a text about the grounds for divorce. It is very typical of rabbinic law to begin with all the details, and only afterwards to explain the principles behind the law. So the following text is the very last mishnah in *Gittin*:

39   *Mishnah Gittin 9.10*

The School of Shammai say, A man is not to divorce his wife unless he has found in her some indecency, as it is said (Deut. 24.1), 'Because he has found some indecency in her.' But the School of Hillel say, Even if she spoiled the cooking, as it is said 'Because he has found some indecency in her.' Rabbi Akiva says, Even if he has found another more beautiful than she is, as it is said (Deut. 24.1) 'And it shall come to pass, if she does not find favour in his eyes.'

This mishnah is very important for the background to the Gospels. Hillel and Shammai may have been still alive when Jesus was born, and their followers ('schools') were disputants of the first century. This dispute is thus contemporary with the Gospel narratives. The School of Shammai normally followed the stricter opinion and Hillel the more lenient opinion: thus here the followers of Shammai are less permissive. The Mishnah quotes the text from Deuteronomy: *erva* is here translated as indecency. But our verse also speaks of 'finding no favour in his eyes'. Is this to be taken as something separate or as something additional? It seems the followers of Shammai would only permit divorce on the grounds of a sexual misdemeanour (adultery or an incestuous relationship), which the woman had entered into outside the marriage. They felt that these were the only reasonable grounds for divorce. It is likely that this particular Mishnah seems to be worded in terms of advice rather than law: other texts suggest that a husband had the legal right from the Torah to divorce his wife whenever he wanted.

The school of Hillel seem to have said something quite different. They appear to be interpreting the phrase *ervat davar* to mean 'even if she spoilt the cooking': and Rabbi Akiva, the second-century rabbi, said 'even if he has found another more beautiful than she' – for any reason at all, just because he wants to, unless he is suggesting that no righteous Jewish man could call another more beautiful than his own wife.

The Rabbis of the Talmud ended their discussion of this mishnah by quoting a saying of Rabbi Yohanan 'He who sends away his wife is hated' (based on Malachi 2.16), and a saying of Rabbi Elazar 'If a man divorces his first wife, even the altar sheds tears' (*Gittin* 90 B). Although the legislation made it very easy for a man to divorce his wife, the influence of such remarks has prevented divorce and remarriage becoming the norm in Jewish family life.

Our discussion has shown that there are no clear grounds for divorce in rabbinic law. Community pressure could prevent people treating divorce lightly: but the interpretation of the grounds for divorce was, except perhaps in cases of adultery, left in the hands of every husband. In other cases there would be no obligation on him to divorce his wife (cf. Matt. 1.18–20). In diaspora communities today, divorce is generally sought in the civil courts first and only afterwards is the *get* issued: Jews living in countries such as Ireland, where there is no civil divorce, cannot get divorced there.

The woman's right to divorce under rabbinic law is a complex matter. The biblical legislation as quoted above clearly contained no provisions for a woman to initiate a divorce action. However, in more modern times rabbinical courts have accepted claims from women for divorce: the difficulty arises that it is incumbent on the husband to write out the divorce document, and to give it to her: but for some hundreds of years it has been considered quite acceptable to compel the husband to do this. The problem arises today that outside Israel rabbinical courts have no real sanctions, and can only operate with the consent of both parties: a recalcitrant husband who does not wish to give his wife a divorce document will not necessarily listen to the rabbinical courts. In Israel it is possible to imprison a husband who refuses to give his wife a divorce document. In Britain there were some interesting cases in the eighteenth and nineteenth centuries which can be read about in James Picciotto's *Sketches of Anglo Jewish History*. There is also a modern work on the woman's right to divorce in Jewish law (*The Jewish Law Annual*, Volume 4, Brill, Leiden 1981). Among the British cases discussed is one in 1969. It concerned a woman who had been awarded a divorce by the civil court but whose husband would not give her a *get*. She appealed to the High Court, pointing out that her divorce was useless to her without the *get* and that her husband's refusal was frustrating the intentions of the court. The court was prepared to use its powers to award maintenance to pressurize the husband, increasing the amount he had to pay if he did not issue a *get*. Within close Jewish communities, it is still possible for moral or business sanctions to be brought on a recalcitrant husband.

The next text is in fact the very next mishnah. It is one of the curiosities of the way rabbinic literature is arranged, that the tractate on divorce comes immediately before the one on marriage. The reason is probably that *Gittin* has more chapters than *Kiddushin*, and the tractates in this part of the Mishnah are arranged with the longest first and the shortest last: but the result of this is that students studying the Talmud today study divorce first, and marriage afterwards. There may well be good psychological reasons for that: it is felt inappropriate to learn about marriage first, and then divorce, but as both have to be studied, it is better to reverse the order.

The name of this next tractate, *Kiddushin*, means 'betrothals', or, more literally, 'consecrations'. The Talmud (*Kiddushin* 2 B) defines betrothal as an act whereby the woman is 'set apart' for her husband, like objects consecrated to the temple (Hebrew *hekdesh*). The title points to the sacred character of marriage in rabbinic thought.

This first *mishnah* describes how betrothal takes place. Betrothal in rabbinic law means a firm agreement to marry, which cannot be broken off without a divorce.

40   *Mishnah Kiddushin 1.1*

A woman is acquired in three ways and she acquires herself [again] in two ways. She is acquired by money, by document, or by intercourse. By money – the School of Shammai say, by a *dinar* or something of the same value as a *dinar*: but the School of Hillel say, by a *perutah*, or something of the same value as a *perutah*. And how much is a *perutah*? one-eighth of an Italian *issar*. And she acquires herself [again] by divorce, or by the death of her husband.

Notice the phrase 'acquires herself'. Before the time of Shimon ben Shetah, we learned, a divorced woman was to some extent dependent on her father. The phrasing here, however, perhaps suggests a certain degree of independence.

Betrothal by intercourse was considered to be implied by various texts in the Torah, but in later times this method was prohibited by rabbinical decree as indecent. As for betrothal by document, there is a great deal of modern dispute among scholars as to precisely what was the document mentioned in this mishnah: the standard modern work on this subject is Epstein's *The Jewish Marriage Contract*. He suggests that the document mentioned here is not the *ketubah*, but a separate document which he calls the *shetar kiddushin* or betrothal contract. In rabbinic times the agreement to marry was normally several years before the wedding, and it was quite normal for young girls to be betrothed, who would marry only much later on with their consent, once they had reached the age of majority. A betrothal is binding in rabbinic law. This contrasts with Christian tradition in which the question of divorce would not arise until marriage.

In mishnaic times or even earlier, betrothal by document had ceased to be common, and betrothal was normally by a gift of money. No contract can be completed without a financial value being involved. We see a dispute in the Mishnah about the amount of money required: it was the opinion of the School of Hillel which prevailed, which meant in effect that the smallest possible coin would suffice. However, the small gift of money was subsequently often replaced by the gift of a ring. So this mishnah gives the origin of the wedding ring in Jewish tradition. The ring has to belong to the bridegroom, and he gives it to the bride as the symbol of the *perutah*, the small coin of the Mishnah. The value of the ring is therefore of some importance, and so it is still part of rabbinic legislation that it should be plain and unadorned, so that its value is clear.

In the Gospels, there are two parallel texts on divorce, in Matthew and Mark. There is a remarkable difference between the two texts. Christian tradition tends to be selective in the parts of the Gospels it remembers: many Christians remember only the Gospel passage in which Jesus does not allow divorce under any circumstances. Here is an area of great controversy, first, because it raises the question of how literal one can be in interpreting texts which flatly contradict each other – selective quoting disguises such contradictions – and secondly, because it has repercussions for contemporary Christian practice. If the teaching of Jesus is quite clear, then any shift in established practice is very difficult: but if there is ambiguity in the Gospels' interpretation of the teaching of Jesus, this can make it easier for attitudes to change.

41   *(i) Matthew 19.1–14*

[1]Now when Jesus had finished these sayings, he went away from Galilee and entered the region of Judea beyond the Jordan; [2]and large crowds followed him, and he healed them there. [3]And Pharisees came up to him and tested him by asking, 'Is it lawful to divorce one's wife for any cause?' [4]He answered, 'Have you not read that he who made them from the beginning made them male and female, [5]and said, "For this reason a man shall leave his father and mother and be joined to his wife, and the two shall become one flesh"? [6]So they are no longer two but one. What therefore God has joined together, let not man put asunder.' [7]They said to him, 'Why then did Moses command one to give a certificate of divorce, and to put her away?' [8]He said to them, 'For your hardness of heart Moses allowed you to divorce your wives, but from the beginning it was not so. [9]And I say to you: whoever divorces his wife, except for unchastity, and marries another, commits adultery.'

[10]The disciples said to him, 'If such is the case of a man with his wife, it is not expedient to marry.' [11]But he said to them, 'Not all men can receive this saying, but only those to whom it is given. [12] For there are eunuchs who have been so from birth, and there are eunuchs who have been made eunuchs by men, and there are eunuchs who have made themselves eunuchs for the sake of the kingdom of heaven. He who is able to receive this, let him receive it.'

[13]Then children were brought to him that he might lay his hands on them and pray. The disciples rebuked the people; [14]but Jesus said, 'Let the children come to me, and do not hinder them; for to such belongs the kingdom of heaven.'

(ii) Mark 10.1–14

[1]And he left there and went to the region of Judea and beyond the Jordan, and crowds gathered to him again; and again, as his custom was, he taught them.

[2]And Pharisees came up and in order to test him asked, 'Is it lawful for a man to divorce his wife?' [3]He answered them, 'What did Moses command you?' [4]They said, 'Moses allowed a man to write a certificate of divorce, and to put her away.' [5]But Jesus said to them, 'For your hardness of heart he wrote you this commandment. [6]But from the beginning of creation, "God made them male and female." [7]For this reason a man shall leave his father and mother and be joined to his wife, [8]and the two shall become one flesh. So they are no longer two but one. [9]What therefore God has joined together, let not man put asunder.'

> [10]And in the house the disciples asked him again about this matter. [11]And he said to them, 'Whoever divorces his wife and marries another, commits adultery against her; [12]and if she divorces her husband and marries another, she commits adultery.'
> [13]And they were bringing children to him, that he might touch them; and the disciples rebuked them. [14]But when Jesus saw it he was indignant.

Some details of the text are worth considering. Both state that the Pharisees came up 'to test him'. This can mean that they were trying to find out what his views were: the word in itself need not necessarily be a hostile one, but its frequent use in the Gospels does tend to suggest an atmosphere of antagonism and hostility, as well as debate. In Matthew they ask the question 'Is it lawful to divorce one's wife for any cause?' These last three words are not in Mark. The phrase 'for any cause' is in Greek *kata pasan aitian* – *pasan* means 'each' or 'every'. Perhaps they were not asking 'Are there any circumstances in which divorce is permitted?', but asking Jesus to give what in his opinion were the grounds for divorce. With this interpretation, the sentence should be translated 'Is it lawful to divorce one's wife for *every* reason?' This would mean that Jesus was being drawn into the contemporary debate between the school of Hillel and the school of Shammai on the permissible grounds for divorce. Now in the rabbinic legislation the possibility of divorce was an important factor in the wedding itself, in the clauses of the *ketubah*: perhaps here also they were trying not so much to define the conditions under which a marriage could be dissolved, but the conditions of the marriage contract: the more difficult it is to end a contract, the more weight and responsibility is attached to entering one. Through the discussion of grounds for divorce, the early Christians may have been attempting to tighten the definition of the contract of marriage. Where marriage is easy to dissolve, frequent marrying is a relatively easy matter. Where divorce is difficult, marriage is permanent. The discussion is not only about divorce, but about the sacredness of the idea of marriage, and its permanence. It becomes a question of commitment.

It is interesting to consider Jesus' reply in the light of the rabbinic texts studied. The quotations from Genesis given by Jesus are certainly ones the rabbis considered apt when talking about marriage – Adam and Eve are often cited as an ideal of monogamous marriage. But a rabbi would have difficulty with the phrase which follows 'What therefore God has joined together, let not man put asunder.' This is because the passage from Deuteronomy, about divorce, is also considered to be from God. The Pharisees make this point. They would not have agreed with Jesus' contention that there existed an earlier time when there was no divorce, even though divorce is not mentioned in Genesis. The phrase in Matthew 19.7 and Mark 10.4 for 'certificate of divorce', (*Biblion apostasiou*), is very close to sefer *keritut* in Deuteronomy. In fact it is the Septuagint translation of these words.

In Mark's version, note how Jesus replies 'It was for your hardness of heart (*sklerokardia*) that Moses allowed you to divorce'. It is sometimes stated in rabbinic arguments that God gave various laws as a concession to man's weakness. For example, in modern times, many have argued that Genesis states that man was created vegetarian, but God allowed Noah and his descendants to eat meat as they could not manage without.[2] If divorce could be regarded as a similar kind of concession, it would therefore follow that it would be better if there were no divorce. The question then arises of how strong people are. Are they able to do without it, or are they still too weak? Rabbinic thought more often regards subsequent generations as gradually getting worse, rather than better, and requiring more concessions rather than requiring less.[3]

Notice how the wording of Matthew and Mark have slight differences throughout except for one part which is almost exactly the same – verses 4–6 in Matthew and 6–9 in Mark, which includes the unrabbinic notion 'What therefore God has joined together, let not man put asunder.' Perhaps it was a saying with a fixed status before the Gospels were written. It stands out as an emphatic statement.

Mark gives a clear statement that divorce is not permitted under any circumstances. There seems no doubt that his community prohibited divorce: perhaps they thought marriage had reached a stage of being a commitment forever: this was a departure from rabbinic tradition. If, as most think, Mark was written earlier, it makes the Matthew passage all the more interesting. Against the background of a fixed statement by Mark that divorce was not acceptable, Matthew presents that fixed statement in a totally new way. This is more than a slight discrepancy between texts, but a flat contradiction of one community by another. For Christians, the revelation of God can contain and hold disagreements, just as rabbinic literature can.

It seems likely that for the earliest Christians these were the last days, the apocalyptic period, and they echo the time before – 'from the beginning it was not so'. Therefore divorce was in a sense irrelevant for their communities. Paul writes that the unmarried should not marry, the married not divorce in the crisis of the time (see I Cor. 7.26). They seem to have thought of the end coming very rapidly: but as time passed and the communities discovered that the end had not arrived, they must have returned to normal living: Matthew, then, reflects later thinking. He and his community were very concerned with the sense of how, with the knowledge of the new era, they could nevertheless return to day-to-day living. The passage is typical of Matthew and his main themes.

Does Jesus speak his views openly or secretly? The command in Matthew seems to be given in the presence of the Pharisees, but in Mark it is only to the disciples.

One interpretation of Jesus' reply in Matthew 19.9 would point to the parallels with the Deuteronomy verse. According to this interpretation, the phrase 'except for unchastity' (*porneia*) is a reasonable translation of the word *erva* which we find in Deuteronomy. It is important to consider in more detail the meaning of this term *porneia*, since this is obviously crucial to a discussion of Christian divorce. The dictionary meanings[4] are prostitution, unchastity, fornication, referring to every kind of unlawful sexual intercourse – a clear equivalent to the Hebrew term *erva*. Some commentators, however, avoid the issue by stating that it is impossible to know exactly what it means, whereas others try to reconcile it with the text in Mark, by stating it refers only to incest: in a case of incest, the marriage would be totally invalid, and the ending of such a relationship would not count as divorce. But the basic meaning of the Greek word can cover any form of unlawful sexual intercourse, like the Hebrew term. It is the closest Greek equivalent for the Hebrew term, even though the root of *erva* comes from nakedness, *porneia* from prostitution. For this reason some commentators have linked it with the Hebrew word for prostitution, *zenut*.

Bauer's dictionary gives some examples, including to be born from *porneia* = to be illegitimate. He refers to Genesis 38.24, 'harlotry', where in the Septuagint, the word does seem to translate *zenut*. However, this refers to the story of Judah and Tamar. Tamar had in fact pretended to be a prostitute, but the word has additional force here, because Tamar should have gone through a levirate marriage (see Deut. 25.5–10) with her brother-in-law, and Judah had told her to wait for him. For her to contract another relationship was adultery, even if she had not played the prostitute. There are other sources where *porneia* can refer to the adultery of a married woman, although it is not the usual word for it. It would seem incorrect to restrict the meaning of the word to 'incest' as some commentators do, saying the relationship should not be continued because it should never have existed. Matthew's discussion of divorce cannot be dismissed so easily: it is much closer to the rabbinic view.

The sequence in Matthew 19.9 is significant: it does not simply talk of divorce but remarriage. Jesus links divorce with remarriage, and it is also so linked in Deuteronomy, where the text goes on to speak of remarriage. Now rabbinic legislation does not draw a necessary link between divorce and remarriage: it was permitted to divorce even if one did not intend to remarry, and there is much in rabbinic texts that is close to the modern view that the breakdown of a marriage is sufficient grounds for a divorce, even if neither of the parties wishes to remarry. But it does seem that both in Matthew and Mark it is not the separation of husband and wife which is at issue, but the freedom to remarry. In the Catholic Church this is still the issue: the church has never forbidden separation, but held that divorce does not leave a person free to remarry, and only very recently has the Church of England permitted some divorcees to remarry in church.

There is much work to be done in Christian theology on this: it is the legitimacy of remarriage which is the point at issue. In both of the Gospel texts, the concept of adultery is also different from that of the rabbis. In rabbinic law it is only the married woman and her partner who commit adultery, but in these texts both the man and the woman equally. Maybe there is a confusion, and the Gospel intends to refer to the woman who remarries, or perhaps the texts are stating that the same definition of adultery now applies to men and women – a significant redefinition. This step is particularly noticeable in Mark, and many have pointed to it as evidence of a Roman background, where women's rights were different. Also, Mark then speaks of a woman divorcing her husband: does that imply he was living in a situation where that was possible? Or does it imply a wish to widen the freedom to divorce? The wording seems to suggest this was the practice where the Gospel was being written.

In verse 13 of Matthew there begins a passage which also has a parallel in Luke (18.15–17). In both Matthew and Mark this passage comes straight after the discussion of divorce – and it significantly deals with children – 'to such belongs the kingdom of heaven'. Matthew does not use a consistent logical development, but often a word or phrase or idea in one story leads on to the next theme. So here divorce leads him to write about children.

Notice too the strange discussion in Matthew 19.12 about eunuchs. If for Matthew's community the real issue was not divorce but somehow trying to strengthen the commitment to marriage, such debate would be bound to raise the question, that if marriage is going to be as difficult as that, does it make sense to take it on? This may have been part of the discussion: 'If such is the case of a man with his wife, it is not expedient to marry.' This mirrors the rabbinic debate discussed above (in the discussion of text 37, p. 123), that when divorce was too easy, they did not want to marry. It must have been a subject of current debate. If divorce was too easy, then the women would not want to get married: if too difficult, the men would not want to get married: it was always important to try to strike a balance, in order to preserve and safeguard the institution of marriage.

Christian tradition is that Jesus himself did not marry. This is in fact a deduction from silence: it is not explicitly stated in the Gospels that he was not married. In rabbinic texts, however, an argument from silence would suggest the reverse: it was so unusual for rabbis not to marry that such a fact would probably have been mentioned. Thus a Jew reading the Gospels might assume that Jesus was married, a Christian that he was not. A shift of perspective has taken place – perhaps in the period of the desert fathers, cutting themselves off from life, by imitation in living death of the kind of death Jesus had actually died – a kind of assumption in the development of Christianity that there is an ideal greater than marriage, whereas in the Jewish tradition this would be very unusual.

Thus we can conclude that Jewish and Christian teachings on divorce began and developed differently, remain different, and have always been recognized as being so. There is, however, in Matthew's use of the word *porneia* a fascinating hint that the differences may not be quite so great as they may at first appear.

Who Can Forgive?

Initial point of comparison:
Theological

The aims of this final unit are:

1. To compare and contrast Gospel and rabbinic attitudes to repentance and forgiveness, with particular emphasis on the question 'Who is empowered to grant forgiveness?'

2. To show how modern controversies and dialogues on the theme of 'forgiveness' still reflect the differences to be found in the ancient texts.

The reader of this unit will find it helpful to watch for the way the terms 'forgiveness' and 'repentance' are used with different emphases in the two traditions, and should take particular care when translating ancient terms into modern ones, and Hebrew terms into English ones.

The comparison of texts in this final unit encapsulates one of the most difficult issues in Jewish-Christian dialogue today. This issue has already been mentioned in previous units: it is now time to consider it in more detail. The issue can be summarized as follows: many Gospel texts refer to Jesus in terms which rabbinic texts would use only for God. This reflects a very basic difference between Judaism and Christianity which still causes difficulties for many.

Teshuvah

The word used in rabbinic Hebrew for repentance is *teshuvah*, which comes from a root meaning 'return'. A person who sins is considered to be far from God, and the repentant sinner returns to God. Buber called repentance in Judaism 'the decisive turning point in a man's life'. That God looks for and accepts the truly penitent is an idea frequently found in the Hebrew prophets: for example, Malachi 3.7:

> Return unto Me, and I will return unto you, says the Lord of Hosts.

In rabbinic tradition, in order to repent, the penitent should first seek to make amends for what he has done wrong: a thief must give back what he has stolen: if somebody has caused injury, he must pay for the medical treatment. The idea of making amends is a basic prerequisite for the forgiveness of sins between people. It is with that background that we turn to this passage:

42 *Tosefta Baba Metsia 8.26*

For tax-collectors and publicans repentance is difficult; they are to give back [the money] to those they are aware of, and as for the rest, he is to use it for public requirements.

This is a practical *halakhah*: tax collectors were at this time entrepreneurs who hired from the Roman government the right to collect the taxes for a specific area: if they had dishonestly taken too much tax it would be very difficult to return it all: they would not have kept records from whom the money came. They could be in a situation where they wished to make amends, but were unaware of the source of their ill-gotten gains. Therefore the *Tosefta* suggests that the money should be given to charity.

In Luke, chapter 19, the story is told of how Jesus went as a guest to the house of a tax-collector called Zacchaeus (Luke 19.8):

And Zacchaeus stood and said to the Lord, 'Behold, Lord, the half of my good I give to the poor; and if I have defrauded any one of anything, I restore it fourfold.'

Zacchaeus' repentance in this story is marked by his making amends in the way prescribed in the rabbinic text.

The following text takes the idea a little further:

43 *Mishnah Avot 5.18 (in some editions 5.21)*

Whoever causes the multitude to be righteous, through him no sin shall be brought about; but he who causes the multitude to sin shall not have the means to repent.

This text from 'Sayings of the Fathers' concerns a person who leads a community or has influence in public life. The context is important here: the previous paragraph makes a distinction between a controversy which is for the sake of heaven, which it states is of lasting worth, and a controversy which is not for God's sake, which is of no lasting worth. The Mishnah gives as an example of a controversy for the sake of heaven, the disputes of Hillel and Shammai: and of the other sort, a misplaced controversy, conducted out of spite and jealousy, the controversy of

Korah and his company (Num. 16). Our text follows immediately, and again examples are given: Moses is mentioned as an example of a leader who led people to be righteous, Jereboam of one who led man to sin.

So the position of a community leader was considered to be particularly important – if he acts wrongly repentance is beyond him. This phrase should also be regarded in practical terms: how is it that somebody who has led many astray can make amends? There is no easy way in which he can make up for what he has done: so the rabbis suggest that he is in a particularly difficult position. Repentance would be out of his hands, suggests our text, while those he has led astray are still held responsible for the wrong he has taught them.

When a person has made amends to his fellow, the next stage is for him to repent and confess his sins before God. This process is particularly associated with the *Yom Kippur*, the Jewish fast day and Day for Atonement which takes place in the autumn. In the Jewish calendar, this day comes as the culmination of a period of searching and repentance: the days immediately leading up to and including *Yom Kippur* are known as the 'Ten Days of Penitence', and these ten days begin with *Rosh HaShanah*, the Jewish New Year. The idea is that the prior repentance and the public confession on *Yom Kippur* absolve from sins against God: when the sin is against man, restitution is also a necessary prerequisite.

Mekhilta on Exodus 20.7 **44**

'For the Lord will not hold him guiltless who takes his name in vain.' Rabbi Elazar says 'It is impossible to say "He will not hold guiltless" (Ex. 34.7), since it has already stated "To hold guiltless" (do.) But it is impossible to say "To hold guiltless", since it is also said "He will not hold guiltless". Say therefore: he holds guiltless those who repent, but he does not hold guiltless those who do not repent.'

This passage forms a comment on a verse from the Ten Commandments which prohibits taking God's name in vain, 'for the Lord will not hold him guiltless' – the Hebrew verb could also be translated 'clear' or 'acquit'. Rabbi Elazar, who lived in the second century CE and was a contemporary of Rabbi Akiva, compares a text from Exodus 34.7. This second text cannot be clearly understood from an English translation. It forms part of a narrative in which Moses experiences a vision of God's glory. According to rabbinic tradition, this event actually took place on *Yom Kippur*: for on that day the Jewish people were forgiven for the sin of worshipping the golden calf (Ex. 32). The relevant Hebrew phrase reads *venakkeh lo yenakkeh*. This is grammatically an infinitive followed by a finite verb, which is an idiomatic way of expressing emphasis in Hebrew. The phrase thus means 'he will surely not acquit the guilty'. By splitting the phrase into two, however, Rabbi Elazar makes it mean 'To hold guiltless he will not hold guiltless' – a phrase which makes no sense as it stands. It enables him, however, to make his own *midrash*, interpreting the text to mean that God lets off the repentant, but he does not acquit those who are not repentant. The community by fasting, prayer and confession on the Day for Atonement, makes atonement for its sins and is forgiven by God.

If people are to be so easily forgiven, will they not be tempted to act rashly? The rabbis thought of this difficulty, and answered as follows:

45   *Mishnah Yoma 8.9*

If somebody said 'I will sin and repent, and sin again and repent,' he will be given no opportunity to repent. [If he said,] 'I will sin and *Yom Kippur* will effect atonement,' then *Yom Kippur* effects no atonement. For transgressions that are between man and God *Yom Kippur* effects atonement, but for transgressions that are between man and man *Yom Kippur* effects atonement only if he has appeased his fellow. . . .
Said Rabbi Akiva: Happy are you, Israel. Before whom are you made clean and who makes you clean? Your father in heaven . . .

This is part of the last mishnah in Tractate *Yoma*, the section of the Mishnah about *Yom Kippur*, the Day for Atonement. The first statement here shows the concern of the rabbis that the day should not be regarded as an automatic path to absolution: the public confessions uttered on that day are to be regarded as important, but not sufficient in themselves: otherwise, somebody might think about this in advance and do something wrong, on the assumption that he could make up for it afterwards.

The second statement was interpreted to mean that a peson who has wronged somebody else must make amends and restitution to him, as described above. The text shows clearly that this is part of the process of repentance. Forgiveness, in the sense of letting go of anger and resentment, is to be seen as part of this systematic process of repentance: forgiveness comes from God, as the book of Leviticus states in connection with *Yom Kippur* (Lev. 16.30):

> For on that day. . . . from all your sins before the Lord you shall be clean.

Rabbi Akiva's words in our mishnah emphasize that forgiveness comes from God: they could perhaps even be taken to mean that any remaining human resentment for one's sins does not matter, if one has made amends and properly repented: what matters is the much more important assurance of God's forgiveness. Rabban Gamaliel, however, is reported to have said that God grants mercy when man is merciful, and does not grant mercy when man is not merciful.[1] There is no suggestion in the rabbinic thought of our period that human forgiveness should precede repentance: both are part of a single process.

The first Gospel texts appear at first sight to present a very different tone:

(i) Matthew 12.31–32   46

[31]Therefore I tell you, every sin and blasphemy will be forgiven men, but the blasphemy against the Spirit will not be forgiven. [32]And whoever says a word against the Son of man will be forgiven; but whoever speaks against the Spirit will not be forgiven, either in this age or in the age to come.

(ii) Mark 3.28–30

[28]'Truly, I say to you, all sins will be forgiven the sons of men, and whatever blasphemies they utter; [29]but whoever blasphemes against the Holy Spirit never has forgiveness, but is guilty of an eternal sin' – [30]for they had said, 'He has an unclean spirit.'

(iii) Luke 12.10

And every one who speaks a word against the Son of man will be forgiven; but he who blasphemes against the Holy Spirit will not be forgiven.

These texts centre on what, for the Christian community, presented an apparently total block to repentance. Here the problem does not seem to be about making amends to fellow human beings but to God. So they seem to present a totally different view from the rabbinic passages. There may, however, be some connection. The rabbis categorized various offences, such as those of the community leader or tax collector, whose very nature made repentance difficult. In other cases, they thought, repentance was made difficult because the offender did not think there was anything to repent for. Perhaps here the same issues are being discussed. We can make amends for what we have done to other people, but how can we make up for what we have done against God? Because we cannot make amends, we cannot properly repent, and because we cannot properly repent, we cannot be forgiven or pardoned. Or, if forgiveness is achieved in returning to God, how can this be done by an individual who despises (a possible meaning for *blasphemia*) God's Spirit and sees no value in repentance?

The Gospels, however, seem to go further than this. In Matthew's account, the context makes it clear that 'the Spirit' refers to the 'spirit of God' which is present in Jesus. Jesus is debating with the Pharisees whether he heals through 'the spirit of God', or through some demonic force. Matthew prefaces his account with a quotation from Isaiah (42.1):

> I will put my Spirit upon him,
> and he shall proclaim justice to the Gentiles.

The 'sin' seems to be the denial of the presence of God's spirit claimed by Jesus and by the Christian community.

The term 'blasphemy' in these Gospel texts is a Greek term difficult to translate into rabbinic terms. The context here suggests that it is some offence against God which is clearly distinguishable from offences against human beings, but it is difficult to be more precise than this. One definition given in modern dictionaries is 'evil or disparaging speech'. Here the rabbinic texts may again be helpful. According to Mishnah Avot (text 43, p. 140),

> he who causes the multitude to sin
> shall not have the means to repent.

Could it be that the evangelists are attacking those (including Christians) whose speech or behaviour leads others to deny that God's spirit worked in Jesus and in his community?

The passage, viewed in this way, seems to treat as unforgivable a complete denial of everything which is at the heart of the Christian's faith in Jesus, something so central that it is impossible to understand how it could be forgiven. The Gospels were written at a time when the separate communities were becoming hostile to each other, and a great deal of bitterness can be seen in the writing: something which denies the spirit of the faith which the followers of Jesus have, is seen by them to be quite unforgivable.

As we have seen, some rabbinic texts suggest that *any* sin can be forgiven: others list transgressions too serious for ultimate forgiveness. The most well known of these is Mishnah *Sanhedrin* 10.1, quoted in Unit One (text 9, p. 32). This text states that all Israel shall have a share in the world to come – and then it proceeds to list those people who will not. Included in the list is this statement: 'Abba Saul (second century) said: Also he who pronounces the name of God with its proper letters.' This is a possible Jewish equivalent of the Greek term 'blasphemy'.

Another part of this mishnah may possibly be directed against Christians. Rabbi Akiva included among those who do not have a share in the world to come 'he who reads heretical books, or utters charms over a wound and says, "I will put none of the disease upon you which I have put upon the Egyptians: for I am the Lord who heals you"' (Ex. 15.26). The phrase 'heretical books' is thought to be a reference to books excluded from the canon of the Hebrew Bible. The Exodus quotation shows that he who utters charms over a wound would mean he who puts himself in the place of God – as Jesus seems to in a number of Gospel stories.

The polemic in this mishnah is similar to that in the Gospel texts in its implied attack on various sectarian or unorthodox groups. The suggestion that they will not share in the world to come seems to be more a threat made by men than a promise from God. Matthew seems to make a similar threat, when he quotes 'either in this age or in the age to come'. Seen from either side, rejection is unforgivable.

One might well ask how there could be an unforgivable sin if one is in ignorance – as most non-Christians cannot fully comprehend the reality of the faith of those who believe in Jesus. Surely one can only sin when one knows what it is one is doing wrong. However, when something is crystal clear and obvious to you, it can sometimes be difficult to believe that it is not just stubbornness which is making somebody else refuse it – it is sometimes difficult to credit the good faith of somebody who does not see what you see. The early Christian communities were fighting with each other about what was important to them, and their animosities were all too human.

It is worth pointing out that the human element in the composition of the Gospels is officially recognized by the Catholic Church (*Dogmatic Constitution on Divine Revelation*, Vatican II, *Dei Verbum*, 18 November 1965 (paragraphs 11 and 12):

> To compose the sacred books, God chose certain men who, all the while he employed them in this task, made full use of their powers and faculties. . . .
>
> Seeing that, in sacred Scripture, God speaks through men in human fashion, it follows that the interpreter of sacred Scriptures, if he is to ascertain what God has wished to communicate to us, should carefully search out the meaning which the sacred writers really had in mind . . . the exegete must look for that meaning which the sacred writer, in a determined situation and given the circumstances of his time and culture, intended to express . . .

Thus the writers of the Gospels as well as all the scriptures are human authors in the fullest sense of the word: if we are to understand the word of God speaking through them, we must first understand the human elements of the composition. Only through that can we hear God speaking. The fact that there is a human element and human prejudice within the writings is not an obstacle but the vehicle through which we hear the word of God. Controversy and fighting is the process through which all the early Councils of the church went to discover the meaning of God.

In that whole painful process of communities fighting each other, we can each discover something about our faith and its importance – not just about what we believe, but how we can relate to each other, and the dangers which can result from our beliefs. It is only if we understand the polemical elements in the texts that it becomes possible for us to live side by side as believing communities, with an understanding of the richness of other faiths, and what God has communicated to them.

Our final text is Matthew 9.1–9. Parallel texts are Mark 2.1–14 and Luke 5.17–28.

47 *Matthew 9.1–9*

And getting into a boat he crossed over and came to his own city. [2]And behold, they brought to him a paralytic, lying on his bed; and when Jesus saw their faith he said to the paralytic, 'Take heart, my son; your sins are forgiven.' [3]And behold, some of the scribes said to themselves, 'This man is blaspheming.' [4]But Jesus, knowing their thoughts, said, 'Why do you think evil in your hearts? [5]For which is easier, to say, "Your sins are forgiven," or to say "Rise and walk"? [6]But that you may know that the Son of man has authority on earth to forgive sins' – he then said to the paralytic – 'Rise, take up your bed and go home.' [7]And he rose and went home. [8]When the crowds saw it, they were afraid, and they glorified God, who had given such authority to men.

[9]As Jesus passed on from there, he saw a man called Matthew sitting at the tax office; and he said to him, 'Follow me.' And he rose and followed him.

An analysis of this text could well begin by trying to answer Jesus' unanswered question – Which *is* easier to say: 'Your sins are forgiven' or 'Rise and walk'? Surely it is easier to *say* 'your sins are forgiven' – who can prove it? Jesus took the more difficult path of healing the man's paralysis. And so the miracle seems to be used as proof of the forgiveness. Otherwise, how would one prove forgiveness? Jesus manipulates the request for healing as a way of making visible an invisible idea – that the 'Son of man has authority on earth to forgive sins'. In both the forgiving and the healing, it is Jesus who makes the statements and issues the commands – the role one might well expect God to have played.

Rabbinic texts attribute both healing and forgiveness of sins to God. That healing was attributed to God can be seen from the wording of the daily prayer still recited:

Heal us, O Lord, and we shall be healed . . . Grant a perfect healing to all our wounds: for you, God and King, are a faithful and merciful physician.

The precise wording of the last part of the prayer may be of later date: the first part comes from Jeremiah 17.14.

The attribution of healing to God did not mean that Jews in ancient times had no human physicians. On the contrary, the professional medical practitioner is implied as early as the Book of Exodus (21.19). Healing was always a secular profession, never part of the function of a priest.[2] The medicines could be prescribed and applied by man, but the gift of healing is from heaven.

Even today healing often remains a mystery. There is a rehabilitation centre in Britain which is taking a special interest in people with hysterical paralysis: they seem to be able to enable people who have been in wheelchairs for years to walk again. There is also some research being currently carried out at the Institute of Ophthalmology in London into the laying on of hands and faith healing for healing cataracts – halting the progress of a disease which up till now was thought impossible to stop. Faith healers working on this believe the healers have to have faith, but not the patients. Experiments have also been carried out with animals, where one could not say that the animal had faith.

In psychotherapy also the relationship provides a faith within which patients can talk about their anxieties. This Gospel text is one which has much to offer the therapist: we need to free ourselves from our guilt in order to be healed, and a religious faith can help in this process.

In the matter of forgiveness, however, God in the rabbinic tradition has no human agents: 'he holds guiltless those who repent, but he does not hold guiltless those who do not repent.' Certainly it says in our text 'When Jesus saw their faith'. But the faith at issue is that they believe they are going to be made physically well – it is not connected with the forgiveness of sins. The parallel text in Mark gives much more background to the strength of this faith – they were prepared to go to the length of taking the roof off in order to get in.

Perhaps to understand the story fully, the ideas of healing and forgiveness have to be considered together. What is being cured is the attitude: the hope expressed in the passage is comparable to that people today place in medicine: they consult doctors with faith and hope, but sometimes have to accept there may be no physical cure. But in matters of faith things are different: the confidence that sins have been forgiven, that the wounds of the past are healed, restores one's spiritual wholeness, and this can enable a person to shoulder his burdens – to pick up his bed and walk. The evangelist may be saying that spiritual healing takes priority over physical healing.

This Gospel text can be seen to have many different levels of meaning: at one level there is a juxtaposition of a physical cure and a spiritual cure, and of the wonder this caused to people. There is also a debate as to the relationship of physical and spiritual health, and the spiritual health which can carry one through a physical illness. But above all there is the reaction of the crowd, who 'glorified God, who had given such authority to men'. Ultimately, perhaps this text is not about forgiveness at all, but about the *authority* of Jesus.

Note the story of the call of the tax collector in verse 9: it is not difficult to see the connection with the story which precedes. Jesus is once again exercising his authority to forgive. The narrative presents a sharp contrast with the first text studied in this unit, a contrast which throws into relief what is often thought to be one of the main differences between Judaism and Christianity – is salvation to be achieved through good deeds, or through a personal saviour? The truth is that the one idea does not preclude the other: indeed, the two texts could be regarded as part of the same process of repentance, forgiveness and healing for tax collectors. But there is a marked difference of emphasis.

Points for Discussion and Dialogue

When Jews and Christians decide to study together, new insights will be bound to emerge. When Jews and Christians come to study the Gospels together, both will be sensitive to, and discuss, the many passages which refer to Pharisees and Jews. But these are not the only passages which will be found to be disturbing. When Jewish readers find in the Gospels attributes given to Jesus which they associate only with God, there can be a very real sense of shock and confusion. Many Jews ask God daily for healing and forgiveness: in many Gospel passages it is Jesus who heals and forgives. But it is not only these two themes in the Gospels which can carry this sense of shock with them. Compare for example this well known verse in Matthew (10.40)

> He who receives you receives me, and he who receives me receives him who sent me.

with this rabbinic text (*Mekhilta* on Exodus 18.12):

> Everyone who welcomes his fellow-man, it is considered as if he welcomed the Divine Presence.

Again, in *Pirke Avot* 3.2 we read:

> If two sit together, and there are among them words of Torah, the Divine Presence rests between them.

Compare Matthew 18.20:

> For where two or three are gathered in my name, there am I in the midst of them.

Such texts give the impression that Matthew was deliberately usurping things properly said of God for Jesus. But those very familiar with the Gospels may miss this sense of surprise which may well be felt by those approaching them for the first time. It is easy to discuss the academic implications of texts like these – what do the various terms mean, and whether Jesus was divine or not – without being aware of the strong feelings such texts can generate. Add to these feelings a background of two thousand years of Judaism and Christianity developing in contradistinction to each other, and it is hardly surprising that dialogue today is a very difficult enterprise.

One area where the two faiths have developed very differently is in the theology of forgiveness. In Judaism today, as in the texts studied, forgiveness involves making amends to a person wronged, and confessing before God. Asking God's forgiveness is a feature of daily prayers, but fasting and confession are especially associated with *Yom Kippur*. In most Christian theologies, there is no particular *time* associated with forgiveness, but rather a particular *person*. In many Christian denominations, priests hear confessions and grant absolution in accordance with the words of John, in which Jesus is reported as saying to his disciples (John 20.23):

If you forgive the sins of any, they are forgiven.

The idea that the Son of man and his followers have 'authority on earth to forgive sins' is one which is alien and shocking to the rabbinic tradition. From the rabbinic texts studied, the reader will find it easy to see why the scribes in the story found Jesus' remarks blasphemous: in Mark and Luke they say

Who can forgive sins but God alone?

Many Jews reading this passage today find it no easier. The shock of reading such texts can be a profoundly uncomfortable experience.

It is particularly important to understand these sharp differences between Jewish and Christian theology when issues of forgiveness arise which cross the boundaries between the two faiths. In recent years many arguments have taken place about the question of forgiveness for the Holocaust, where some Christian groups have come to Jews and asked for forgiveness, and Jews have replied, in accordance with their tradition, that they can forgive things done to them personally, but they have no power to forgive on behalf of people who have died. This has created and is creating many anxieties in the dialogue world.

In May and June 1985 two controversial articles appeared in *The Times* which provoked a great deal of correspondence.[3] These articles, by Rabbi Dr Albert Friedlander and Anthony Phillips from St John's College Oxford, were on the theme of forgiveness after the Holocaust: and were provoked by a *Times* leader which stated:

> The killing of the Jews in the twentieth century was the final result of a tradition of denigration and rejection of Jews and Judaism dating from early in Christian history, which also tried to strip Jesus of his Jewishness . . .
>
> The problem of evil . . . is not to be solved by some intellectual analysis which makes evil intelligible. The real problem of evil is how it is to be forgiven, and by whom.

In his article, Albert Friedlander wrote of his experiences at a conference in Nuremberg where he had spoken about Auschwitz:

> A young girl rushed up to me after the lecture. 'Rabbi,' she said, 'I wasn't there, but can you forgive me?' and we embraced and cried together.
>
> Then an older man approached me. 'Rabbi,' he said, 'I was a guard at a concentration camp. Can you forgive me?' I looked at him. 'No', I said, 'I cannot forgive. It is not the function of rabbis to give absolution. . . . In Judaism, there is a 10-day period of Penitence, between the New Year and the Day of Atonement, when we try to go to any person whom we have wronged, and ask for forgiveness. But you cannot go to the six million. They are dead, and I cannot speak for them. . . .'

In his reply, Anthony Phillips wrote:

> Without forgiveness there can be no healing within the community . . . In remembering the Holocaust, Jews hope to prevent its recurrence: by declining to forgive, I fear that they unwittingly invite it.

At the heart of this painful debate lay a lack of clarity about the different Jewish and Christian attitudes to forgiveness. This can happen even with people skilled in dialogue when they forget the sources on which the theologies are based. In dialogue the assumptions we make are important. We tend to treat forgiveness as one simple word meaning one thing, but there are different aspects of forgiving: there is the level of internal healing and changing: there is the possibility of making amends: then there is the possibility of being released by the person who has been hurt: there are many different sides to it, and one side may be possible when another is not. The sources can help us to see the question in a much wider and deeper way.

Certainly death can interfere with reconciliation. We can all think of arguments and disagreements which exist in families – and then one of them dies: it leaves the others with a sense of helplessness that things cannot be put right. Forgiveness may not be the answer. What is needed essentially is an inner healing, a coming to terms with the past, a freedom from guilt and fear. The Gospel narratives are profound in the link they draw between healing and freedom from a sense of sin. The rabbinic analysis of the kind of attitudes which block the path back to God is also profound. Yet there is a world of difference between them. Judaism, in its emphasis that forgiveness comes from God, does not permit people to forgive on behalf of others who have been wronged: Christianity explicitly and clearly has given men that function. These are different perspectives which we must understand, because they cannot be harmonized.

Conclusion

This work was started in the belief that it would be interesting to compare rabbinic and Gospel texts, as there had to be a great deal in common between two systems of thought which arose from the same places at the same time. In conclusion, I can point to three very important insights gained from this study.

1. It has become very clear to me that this is one academic field where everybody has an opinion they wish to express. In presenting some of the texts to different groups, I have always found an immediate response. At times, I have found Jewish groups openly hostile to the very idea that they should be asked to look at texts from the Gospels. I have found Christians convinced that all the rabbinic texts must be communicating a message similar to that of Jesus, and others equally certain that their message is very different from anything to be found in Christianity. I have heard reactions which spring from prejudice, reactions based on ignorance, but others too based on great learning or sensitivity – many of which have been incorporated in the discussions here. But above all I have been impressed at how quickly this field of study uncovers real dilemmas which people feel today in their lives – issue of faith and doubt, issues of real concern. For that alone, the work has been worthwhile.

2. Time and again, it has become apparent that texts from the Jewish and Christian sources which appear to deal with the same subject, in fact are discussing and using very different ideas. The phrase 'The Son of man is lord of the sabbath', for example, makes no sense in terms of the halachic debates about details of the permitted and prohibited tasks: that is to say, it is an idea which neither agrees nor disagrees with any particular rabbinic debate, but talks in totally different terms. Much of the scholarly literature on such topics as 'the Sabbath' and 'forgiveness' tries to compare the debates without properly analysing the differences in outlook and terminology. Questions about which text is better

expressed themselves become meaningless when we realize that we are trying to compare two such different systems of thought. Nor do such simplicities as 'Judaism is a religion of Law, Christianity a religion of faith' help at all. Jesus is not portrayed in the Gospels as anti-law, but as discussing quite different matters, no doubt taking for granted the legal basis already in existence. Nor were the rabbis indifferent to matters of faith – but often, they express various individual opinions which are difficult to categorize. In the past, selective quotation of rabbinic texts, and a selective understanding of Gospel texts, has disguised both the similarities of many teachings, and very real differences of theology.

3. Finally, I have come to realize that many of the issues cannot be explored without pain. There is the question of polemic, of the reading and study as 'Gospel truth' of texts hostile or insulting to 'The Jews'. It is the later Gospels which contain more anti-Jewish remarks, as the two faiths became separated and bitterness grew between them. Some Christians are beginning to recognize a need to work on an understanding of Jesus, which says that the presence of Christians in the world can be a blessing for the whole world *without* the whole world being Christian. There is also a need for Jews to be more prepared to study the Gospels, and to speak openly about their shock and concern. Why should we endure that pain? We must, if we are to take our dialogue forward. Fifty years ago, Claude Montefiore was prepared to write and share with Christians his insights on the Gospels in the light of rabbinic teaching. Yet virtually every dialogue group I have myself taken part in, until I began this work, was concerned to explore only themes from Hebrew literature. We encourage Christians to rethink their attitudes to Hebrew literature, but are very reluctant as Jews to enter the world of the Gospels. The conflict we are afraid of is explicitly spelled out in many of the texts. It is not only Christian history which can be understood from those texts, but much of Jewish history as well.

M.H.

Glossary of Hebrew Terms and Rabbinic Literature

Aggadah (also **haggadah**)   Homiletic ethical or narrative literature (opposite of *halakhah*). There are many inconsistencies in *aggadic* material, but there can be only one *halakhah* on a particular subject which is authoritative.

Baraita   Aramaic for 'outside'. A teaching from the period of the *Tannaim* but not included in the *Mishnah*.

CE   Common or Christian era (Jewish way of referring to AD). Note also BCE (Before Common Era).

Halachic Midrash   A literature which uses scripture to provide proof texts for rules of behaviour. The 'principles' of *halachic midrash* are the rules by which scripture is to be interpreted.

Halakhah   The law or the rules of behaviour on a particular subject, as agreed by the rabbis. From this word is derived an English adjective, *halachic*.

Maimonides   Moses ben Maimon (1135–1204). Rabbi, physician, polymath, halachist, commentator, philosopher and writer. Born in Spain, but lived most of his adult life in Cairo.

Mekhilta   A *Tannaitic Midrash* forming a commentary on several chapters from the Book of Exodus, attributed to the disciples of Rabbi Ishmael (died c. 135 CE.) Ishmael's thirteen principles of *Halachic Midrash* (Daily Morning Service: *Baraita de Rabbi Ishmael*) are in opposition to the alternative system of Akiva. Each of the two schools – Ishmael's and Akiva's – is conjectured to have produced a complete set of *Halachic Midrashim*. From Ishmael's school we have *Mekhilta* on Exodus and *Sifre al Bemidbar* – on Numbers.

Midrash   (= enquiry) (i) A homiletic comment or story on a biblical text. (ii) A compilation of such comments on a book of the Bible. (iii) A very large body of rabbinic exegetical, homiletic, and legal literature, which has in common its use of biblical quotation as its basis. It is a completely separate branch of Hebrew literature from *Mishnah* and *Tosefta*.

Mishnah   The most important Rabbinic work of the *Tannaitic* period, compiled around 200 CE, but containing much older material. The opinions of many Jewish teachers are frequently cited by name, teachers dating back to Hillel and Shammai, Jesus' older contemporaries. It is a compilation of Jewish legal material on a huge variety of subjects – ritual, civil, priestly, and everyday – in fact anything subject to rabbinic debate. Conflicting opinions are frequently cited. Contains occasional stories and legends about the Rabbis. About 800 pages in English translation. The Mishnah is divided into six separate sections (orders), and 63 smaller divisions (tractates).

Mitzvah   (Plural **Mitzvot**)   Hebrew for 'Commandment': the word is used for a religious duty or obligation.

Omer   Hebrew for 'sheaf'. (i) The sheaf of barley offered on the second day of Passover (Lev. 23.10); (ii) the fifty days counted from that day until *Shavuot* (Lev. 23.15).

Pesah   The festival of Passover.

Pirke Avot   A tractate of the *Mishnah*, known in English as 'Sayings of the Fathers'.

Rashi   (France, 1040–1105) The most well-known medieval rabbinic commentator on the Bible and Talmud.

Shabbat   Hebrew for 'Sabbath', the weekly day of rest lasting from sunset on Friday to nightfall on Saturday evening.

Shavuot   Hebrew for 'weeks'. The Feast of Weeks, fifty days after the beginning of Passover (Lev. 23.16–21), considered by the rabbis to be the anniversary of the giving of the *Torah* at Sinai.

Shema   Hebrew for 'Hear'. This word denotes the biblical verse 'Hear O Israel, the Lord is our God, the Lord is One' (Deut. 6.4): also the three sections (Deut. 6.5–9; 11.13–20 and Num. 15.37–41) recited twice daily in prayer.

Sifra   A *Tannaitic Midrash* forming a commentary on the Book of Leviticus, attributed to the disciples of Rabbi Akiva (died *c.* 132 CE). Also known as *Torat Cohanim*.

Sifre al Bemidbar   *See* under *Mekhilta*.

Sifre al Devarim   A *Tannaitic Midrash* forming a commentary on the Book of Deuteronomy, attributed to the disciples of Rabbi Akiva (died *c.* 132 CE).

Sukkot   The festival of Tabernacles, also marking the autumn harvest (Lev. 23.39–43).

Talmud   There are two completely separate *Talmuds* – the *Yerushalmi*, written in Palestine, and the *Bavli*, written in Babylon. The second one became authoritative and is the more important. Both contain the *Mishnah*, and voluminous discussions and comments on the Mishnaic material, mainly from the following two centuries (200–400 CE), but some of it older. This discussion is known as the *gemara* (commentary). The older material is in Hebrew, the discussions of the Talmudic period generally in Aramaic. The English translation of the *Bavli* runs to 18 large volumes.

Tannaim/Tannaitic   The teachers/era of the period of the *Mishnah*, approximately 0–200 CE.

Torah   Hebrew for 'teaching'. (i) the Pentateuch (the written *Torah*): (ii) the traditions embodied in the *Mishnah* and *Midrash* and *Talmud* (the oral *Torah*): (iii) the whole body of Jewish religious literature.

Tosefta   A parallel work to the *Mishnah*, arranged in the same sections, but often containing slightly longer . and fuller explanations. Frequently quoted in *Talmud*, but perhaps not known as a complete work in Talmudic times. Its date and purpose are the subject of much scholarly debate, and remain a mystery: however, it is clear that most of the material it contains dates from the Tannaitic period.

Notes

Introduction

1. The view here given of the origin of the title Rabbi broadly follows that put forward by Solomon Zeitlin in two articles in *Jewish Quarterly Review* (*JQR*), Vols. 53 and 59 (full titles are in the Bibliography). These articles were written in reply to two articles by Hershel Shanks, which appeared in the same volumes. Shanks denied that the title was anachronistic in the time of Jesus, but he relied very much on the use of the word *rav* in the Bible, rather than the much closer and more relevant rabbinic evidence.

2. See Raymond Brown, *The Community of the Beloved Disciple*, 1979, and Fr Robert Murray's article 'Jews, Hebrews and Christians; Some Needed Distinctions', 1982.

Unit One

1. See H. Denzinger, *Enchiridion Symbolorum*, Para. 609 (Nicea II, 787), Para. 1501 (Trent, 1546), and Para. 3006 (Vatican I, 1870).

2. Segal, *Two Powers in Heaven*, gives a very thorough account of the relevant texts.

3. See Davies, *The Setting of the Sermon on the Mount*, pp. 245–6.

4. Sanders, *Paul and Palestinian Judaism*, p. 150 ff.

5. Palestinian Talmud, *Peah* 15B (*Halakhah* 1.1) – decree reported by Rabban Gamaliel II.

Unit Two

1. The fourteenth century scholar Aburdaham related the origin of the *haftarot* to the persecution under Antiochus Epiphanes in the second century BCE. A more modern view of the origin of the *haftarot* can be read in S. Safrai, 'The Synagogue', in Safrai and Stern 1976, pp. 908–944.

2. See Raymond Brown, *The Birth of the Messiah*, pp. 166, 207, 514–515.

3. J. T. Sanders, *The Jews in Luke-Acts*, p. 165.

Unit Three

1. Joachim Jeremias, *The Parables of Jesus*, p. 12.

2. See Saul Lieberman, *Greek in Jewish Palestine*, for a discussion of the Greek background.

3. For an explanation of the term *Targum*, see Unit Two, p. 43.

Unit Four

1. I follow here the explanation of G. Alon, *The Jews in their Land in the Talmudic Age*, Vol. 1, p. 277–285.

Unit Five

1. See Hoenig, 1978, for a full explanation of this and other sources offered for the 39 *melakhot*.

2. This is the halachic background to the ruling of the London *Beit Din* that somebody who finds a burglar in his home on Shabbat is permitted to telephone the police at once (*Jewish Chronicle*, 1 May 1987, *London Extra*, p. 1).

3. G. Vermes, *Jesus the Jew*, Ch. 7, pp. 102–128.

4. G. Alon, *The Jews in Their Land . . .*, Vol. 1, pp. 272–277.

Unit Six

1. See Safrai and Stern, *The Jewish People in the First Century*, Vol. 2, pp. 748 ff.

2. See Louis Berman, *Vegetarianism and the Jewish Tradition*, for a collection of the evidence for this view. There is however no evidence to suggest that the rabbis of the first century used this particular argument about eating meat: the evidence is later.

3. See the statements at the end of Mishnah *Sotah*, especially the following: 'When adulterers multiplied, they discontinued the "bitter waters" (Numbers 5.11–31), and it was Rabban Yohanan ben Zakkai who discontinued it.' (Mishnah *Sotah* 9.9).

4. Walter Bauer, *A Greek-English Lexicon of the New Testament*, p. 693.

Unit Seven

1. Rabban Gamaliel's statement exists in several different versions. I follow the text of the Palestinian Talmud, *Baba Kamma*, Chapter 8, *Halakhah* 10. This version is particularly close to Jesus' words in Matthew 6.14–15: 'For if you forgive men their trespasses, your heavenly Father also will forgive you; but if you do not forgive men their trespasses, neither will your Father forgive your trespasses.'

2. The functions of the priest in respect of 'leprosy' (Leviticus 13) were to examine the patient, to pronounce him 'clean' or 'unclean', and if necessary to isolate him – not to heal or treat the disease (Hyam Maccoby, Leo Baeck College lecture, 16 April 1985).

3. These articles and the resulting correspondence can conveniently be consulted in 'Forgetting and Forgiving: The Post-Bitburg Controversy in Great Britain', *European Judaism*, Vol. 19, No. 2, Spring 1985, pp. 3–17.

Bibliography

A. Primary Sources

Bible

    Torah Neviim Ketuvim, Koren, Jerusalem 1985.

    The Septuagint Version of the Old Testament and Apochrypha With and English Translation and with Various Readings and Critical Notes, Samuel Bagster, London.

    He Kaine Diatheke, Clarendon Press, Oxford 1901.

    The Holy Bible containing The Old and New Testaments Revised Standard Version Translated from the Original Tongues Being the Version Set Forth A.D. 1611 Revised A.D. 1881–1885 and A.D. 1911 Compared with the Most Ancient Authorities and Revised A.D. 1952, Collins, London etc.

Maimonides

    Mishneh Torah, Vol. 2, *Sefer HaMadda*, ed. S. T. Rubinstein, Mossad HaRav Kook, Jerusalem 1972.

Mekhilta

    Mekhilta de-Rabbi Ishmael, ed. and trans. Jacob Z. Lauterbach, 3 volumes, JPSA, Philadelphia, 1933 and reprints.

Midrash Rabbah

    ed. M. A. Mirkin, 11 Volumes, Yavneh, Tel-Aviv, 1971–1977.

Mishnah

    Mishnayot Mevoarot, ed. P. Kahati, 12 vols., Heykhal Shelomo, Jerusalem 1977.

    trans. Herbert Danby, Oxford University Press, London 1933 and reprints.

Prayer Book

    The Authorised Daily Prayer Book of the United Hebrew Congregations of the British Commonwealth of Nations, translated Rev. S. Singer, new edition, Eyre and Spottiswode, London, 1962.

Pseudepigrapha

    The Old Testament: Pseudepigrapha, ed. James H. Charlesworth, London and New York: Vol. 1, 1983; Vol. 2, 1985.

Sifra Debei Rav (Torat Cohanim)

    ed. A. H. Weiss, Vienna 1862.

    pub. Sifra, Jerusalem 1959.

Sifre Al Sefer Bemidbar
ed. H. S. Horovitz, Leipzig 1917.

Sifre Al Sefer Devarim
ed. Louis Finkelstein, Berlin 1939, reprinted JTSA, New York 1969.

Talmud
Babylonian Talmud, 37 tractates, Romm, Vilna, 1886 and reprints.
The Babylonian Talmud, English translation, ed. I. Epstein, 18 volumes Soncino Press, London, Quincentenary edition 1978.
Palestinian Talmud (Yerushalmi), Massekhet Berakhot (with commentaries), ed. G. I. Mirkin, Bnei Brak 1980.

Throckmorton, Burton Jr. (ed.)
Gospel Parallels: A synopsis of the First Three Gospels, Thomas Nelson and Sons, Toronto, Camden NJ and London 1949.

Tosefta
ed. Saul Lieberman, 11 vols., JTSA, New York 1955–1967.

B. Secondary Material

I. Abrahams., *Studies in Pharisaism and the Gospels*, First Series, Cambridge University Press 1917.
Studies in Pharisaism and the Gospels, Second Series, Cambridge University Press 1924.

Gedaliah, Alon, *The Jews in their Land in the Talmudic Age (70–640 C.E.)*, trans. and ed. Gershon Levi, Vol. 1, Magnes Press, Jerusalem 1980.

Sholem, Asch, *The Nazarene*, trans. Maurice Samuel, Routledge & Kegan Paul, London 1939.

Walter Bauer, *A Greek-English Lexicon of the New Testament and Other Early Christian Literature*, adapted, trans. and rev. William F. Arndt and F. Wilbur Gingrich, second edition rev. F. Wilbur Gingrich and Frederick W. Danker, University of Chicago Press, Chicago and London 1958.

Louis A Berman, *Vegetarianism and the Jewish Tradition*, Ktav, New York 1982.

John Bowker, *Jesus and the Pharisees*, Cambridge University Press 1973.

Raymond E. Brown, *The Birth of the Messiah: A Commentary on the Infancy Narratives in Matthew and Luke*, Geoffrey Chapman, London 1977.
The Community of the Beloved Disciple, Geoffrey Chapman, London 1979.

U. Cassuto, *A Commentary on the Book of Exodus*, Hebrew University Magnes Press, Jerusalem, 1967 (first Hebrew ed. 1951).

F. L. Cross (ed.) *The Oxford Dictionary of the Christian Church*, Oxford University Press, London 1957, second ed. 1974.

David Daube, *The New Testament and Rabbinic Judaism*, Arno Press, New York 1973.

W. D. Davies, *The Setting of the Sermon on the Mount*, Cambridge University Press, Cambridge 1966.

Henricus Denzinger (ed.) *Enchiridion Symbolorum: Definitionum et Declarationum de Rebus Fidei et Morum*, 23rd edition, Herder, Frieburg 1963.

Louis Epstein, *The Jewish Marriage Contract: A Study in the Status of the Woman in Jewish Law*, Arno Press, New York 1973 (first pub. 1927).

European Judaism 'Forgetting and Forgiving: the Post-Bitburg Controversy in Great Britain', *European Judaism*, Vol. 19. No. 2, Spring 1985, pp. 3–16.

Gerald Friedlander, *The Jewish Sources of the Sermon on the Mount*, Ktav, New York 1969 (first pub. 1911).

R. Travers Herford, *Christianity in Talmud and Midrash*, Ktav, New York, reprint of ed. of 1903.

Isaac Herzog, *The Main Institutions of Jewish Law*, 2 Volumes, Soncino, London 1967 (first pub. 1931).

Sidney B. Hoenig, 'The Designated Number of Kinds of Labour Prohibited on the Sabbath', *JQR*, Vol. 68, No 4 April 1978 pp. 193–208.

Bernard S. Jackson, *Theft in Early Jewish Law*, Clarendon Press, Oxford 1972.

Louis Jacobs, *What does Judaism Say About...?*, Keter, Jerusalem 1973.

Joachim Jeremias, *The Parables of Jesus*, translated by S. H. Hooke, SCM Press, London, 3rd revised ed. 1972 (first pub. 1954).

Jewish Law Annual, Vol. 4, *The Wife's Right to Divorce*, ed. B. Jackson, Brill, Leiden 1981.

Luke T. Johnson, *The Writings of the New Testament: An Interpretation*, SCM Press, London 1986.

Charlotte Klein, *Anti-Judaism in Christian Theology*, trans. Edward Quinn, SPCK, London 1978.

Samuel Tobias Lachs, *A Rabbinic Commentary on the New Testament: The Gospels of Matthew, Mark and Luke*, Ktav and ADL, New Jersey and New York 1987.

Leo Landman, (ed.), *Messianism in the Talmudic Era*, Ktav, New York 1979.

Pinchas Lapide, *The Resurrection of Jesus: A Jewish Perspective*, translated by Wilhelm C. Linss, SPCK, London 1984.

Saul Lieberman, *Hellenism in Jewish Palestine*, JTS, New York 1950.

Hyam Maccoby, 1973, *Revolution in Judea: Jesus and the Jewish Resistance*, Ocean Books, London 1973.

Hyam Maccoby, *The Day God Laughed: Sayings, Fables and Entertainment of the Jewish Sages*, Robson Books, London 1978.

W. A. Meeks, *The First Urban Christians*, Yale University Press 1983.

C. G. Montefiore, *Rabbinic Literature and Gospel Teachings*, Macmillan, London 1930.

C. G. Montefiore and H. Loewe, *A Rabbinic Anthology*, Schocken, New York 1974 (first pub. 1938).

Robert Murray, 'Jews, Hebrews and Christians: Some Needed Distinctions', *Novum Testamentum*, Vol. 25, No. 3, 1982, pp. 194–208.

R. C. Musaph-Andriesse, *From Torah to Kabbalah: A Basic Introduction to the Writings of Judaism*, SCM Press, London 1973.

Jacob Neusner, *Judaism in the Beginning of Christianity*, SPCK, London 1984.

James Picciotto, *Sketches of Anglo-Jewish History*, new ed. revised Israel Finestein, Soncino, London 1956.

Joseph Rabbinowitz, (ed. and trans.), *Mishnah Megillah*, Oxford University Press, London 1931.

Ellis Rivkin, *A Hidden Revolution*, Abingdon, Nashville 1978.

S. Safrai and M. Stern (eds), *The Jewish People in the First Century: Historical Geography, Political History, Social, Cultural and Religious Life and Institutions*, Vol. 2, ed. S. Safrai and M. Stern, in cooperation with D. Flusser and W. C. van Unnik, Van Gorcum, Assen/Amsterdam 1976 (Compendia Rerum Iudicarum ad Novum Testamentum, Section One).

E. P. Sanders, *Paul and Palestinian Judaism: A Comparison of Patterns of Religion*, SCM Press, London 1977.

Jesus and Judaism, SCM Press, London 1985.

Jack T. Sanders 1987, *The Jews in Luke–Acts*, SCM Press, London 1987.

Samuel Sandmel, *Judaism and Christian Beginnings*, Oxford University Press, New York 1978.

Alan F. Segal, *Two Powers in Heaven: Early Rabbinic Reports about Christianity and Gnosticism*, Brill, Leiden 1977 (Studies in Judaism in Late Antiquity, Vol. 25).

Hershel Shanks, 'Is the Title "Rabbi" Anchronistic in the Gospels?', *JQR*, Vol. 53, Philadelphia, 1962–3, pp. 337–345.

Hershel Shanks, 'Origins of the Title Rabbi', *JQR*, Vol. 59, No. 2, Philadelphia, October 1968, pp. 152–157.

Morton Smith, *Tannaitic Parallels to the Gospels*, (Journal of Biblical Literature, Monograph Series, Volume 6), Society of Biblical Literature, Philadelphia 1951.

Milton Steinberg, *As A Driven Leaf*, Behrman, New York 1939.

Hermann L. Strack and Paul B. Billerbeck, *Kommentar zum Neuen Testament aus Talmud und Midrasch*, C. H. Beck'sche Verlags- buchhandlung, Munich, 7 Vols., 1978 (first pub. 1926)

Hermann L. Strack, *Introduction to the Talmud and Midrash*, Atheneum, New York 1982 (first pub. 1931).

Gerd Theissen, *The Shadow of the Galilean*, SCM Press, London 1987.

Ephraim E. Urbach, *The Sages: Their Concepts and Beliefs*, translated by Israel Abrahams, Two Vols., Hebrew University Magnes Press, Jerusalem 1975.

II Vatican, *Dei Verbum*, 18 November 1965 (trans. Liam Walsh and Wilfred Harrington, as 'Dogmatic Constitution on Divine Revel- ation') in Vatican Council II, ed. Austin Flannery. Dominican Publications, Dublin 1977.

Geza Vermes, *Jesus the Jew: A Historian's Reading of the Gospels*, Collins, London 1973; second edition SCM Press, London 1983.

Solomon Zeitlin, 'A Reply', *JQR*, Vol. 53, Philadelphia, 1962–3, pp. 345–349.

'The Title Rabbi in the Gospels is Anachronistic', *JQR*, Vol. 59, No. 2, Philadelphia, October 1968, pp. 158–160.

Studies in the Early History of Judaism, Vol. 3. Judaism and Christianity, Ktav, New York 1975.

The Rise and Fall of the Judean State: A Political Social and Religious History of the Second Commonwealth, Vol. 3, 66 CE – 120 CE, JPSA, Philadelphia 1978.

Ignaz Ziegler, *Die Königsgleichnisse des Midrasch Beleuchtet Durch die Römische Kaiserzeit*, Breslau 1903.

Selected Bibliography

A. General Works

Bishops Committee for Ecumenical and Interreligious Affairs. *Criteria for the Evaluation of Dramatizations of the Passion*. Washington, D. C.: USCC Publications, 1988.

Croner, Helga, ed. *Stepping Stones to Further Jewish-Christian Relations: An Unabridged Collection of Christian Documents*. Mahwah, NJ: Paulist Press, 1977.

———, ed. *More Stepping Stones to Jewish-Christian Relations: An Unabridged Collection of Christian Documents, 1975–1983*. Mahwah, NJ: Paulist Press, 1985.

——— and Klenicki, Leon, eds. *Issues in the Jewish-Christian Dialogue: Jewish Perspectives on Covenant, Mission and Witness*. Mahwah, NJ: Paulist Press, 1979.

Cunningham, Philip A. *Jewish Apostle to the Gentiles: Paul as He Saw Himself*. Mystic, CT: 23rd Publications, 1986.

Fisher, Eugene. *Faith Without Prejudice*. Mahwah, NJ: Paulist Press, 1977.

———. *Catholics and Jews: What We Have in Common*. Liguori, MO: Liguori Publications, 1987 (24 pp.).

———. *Seminary Education and Christian-Jewish Relations*. Washington, D. C.: National Catholic Educational Assn., 1988.

——— and Klenicki, Leon. *Root and Branches: Biblical Judaism, Rabbinic Judaism and Early Christianity*. Winona, MN: St. Mary's Press, 1987.

———, Rudin, James, and Tanenbaum, Marc. *Twenty Years of Jewish-Catholic Relations*. Mahweh, NJ: Paulist Press, 1986.

——— and Klenicki, Leon, eds. *John Paul II on Jews and Judaism 1979–1985*. Washington, D. C.: NCCB-ADL Publication No. 151–52.

Flannery, Austin, ed. *Vatican Council II: The Conciliar and Post Conciliar Documents*. Northport, NY: Costello Publishing Company, 1975.

Flannery, Edward H. *The Anguish of the Jews: Twenty-Three Centuries of Antisemitism*. Revised Edition. Mahwah, NJ: Paulist Press, 1985.

International Catholic-Jewish Liaison Committee. *Fifteen Years of Catholic-Jewish Dialogue 1970–1985: Selected Papers*. Libreria Editrice Vaticana and Pontifical Lateran University, Rome: 1988.

Heim, S. Mark. *Is Christ the Only Way?* Valley Forge, PA: Judson Press, 1985.

Klenicki, Leon and Huck, Gabe, eds. *Spirituality and Prayer: Jewish and Christian Understandings*. Mahwah, NJ: Paulist Press, 1983.

———— and Wigoder, Geoffrey, eds. *A Dictionary of the Jewish Christian Dialogue*. Mahwah, NJ: Paulist Press, 1984.

Koenig, John. *Jews and Christians in Dialogue: New Testament Foundations*. Philadelphia, PA: Fortress Press, 1983.

Pawlikowski, John T. *What Are They Saying about Christian-Jewish Relations?* Mahwah, NJ: Paulist Press, 1980.

————. *Christ in the Light of the Jewish-Christian Dialogue*. Mahwah, NJ: Paulist Press, 1982.

———— and Wilde, James. *When Catholics Speak about Jews*. Chicago, IL: Liturgy Training Publications, 1986.

Peck, Abraham, ed. *Jews and Christians after the Holocaust*. Philadelphia, PA: Fortress Press, 1982.

Segal, Alan F. *Rebecca's Children: Judaism and Christianity in the Roman World*. Cambridge, MA: Harvard University Press, 1986.

Sloyan, Gerard S. *Jesus in Focus: A Life in Its Setting*. Mystic, CT: 23rd Publications, 1983.

Stendahl, Krister. *Paul Among Jews and Gentiles*. Philadelphia, PA: Fortress Press, 1977.

Van Buren, Paul. *Discerning the Way: A Theology of the Jewish-Christian Reality*. New York, NY: Seabury Press, 1980.

Journals

Christian Jewish Relations. Institute of Jewish Affairs-World Jewish Congress, 11 Herrford Street, London W1Y7DX, England.

Explorations: Rethinking Relationships among Jews and Christians. Newsletter of the American Institute for the Study of Religious Cooperation, 401 North Broad Street, Philadelphia, PA 19108.

Face to Face: An Interreligious Bulletin. Published by the Anti-Defamation League of B'nai B'rith, 823 United Nations Plaza, New York, NY 10017.

Lights on Christian-Jewish Relations. Newsletter of the Office on Christian-Jewish Relations, the National Council of the Churches of Christ is available five times yearly. 475 Riverside Drive, Room 870, New York, NY 10115.

National Dialogue Newsletter. Mr. Frank Brennan, editor. P.O. Box 849, Stamford, CT 06904.

The SIDIC Review (organ of the Service International de Documentation Judeo-Chretienne, Rome) is available quarterly from Dr. Eugene Fisher, Secretariat for Catholic-Jewish Relations, 1312 Massachusetts Avenue, N.W., Washington, D.C. 20005.

B. Rabbinics

Danby, Herbert. *The Mishnah.* Translated from the Hebrew with intro-duction and brief explanatory notes. London: Oxford University Press, 1954.

Holtz, Barry W., ed. *Back to the Sources: Reading the Classic Jewish Texts.* New York, NY: Summit Books, 1984.

The Midrash. Translated into English with notes, glossary and indices under the editorship of Rabbi Dr. H. Freedman and Maurice Simon. In ten volumes. London: The Soncino Press, 1961.

Montefiore, C. G. *Rabbinic Literature and Gospel Teachings.* New York, NY: Ktav Publishing House, Inc., 1970.

—— and Loewe, H., eds. *A Rabbinic Anthology.* Selected and arranged with comments and introductions. New York, NY: Schocken Books, 1974.

Moore, George Foot. *Judaism in the First Centuries of the Christian Era: The Age of the Tannaim.* Cambridge, MA: Harvard University Press, 1962. (Volume I, Section 1, Chapters 1–9).

Neusner, Jacob, ed. *Understanding Rabbinic Judaism from Talmudic to Modern Times.* New York, NY: Ktav-Anti-Defamation League, 1974. (Part 1, Chapters 1 and 2; Part 2, Chapters 3, 4, 5).

Safrai, S. and Stern, M., eds. *Jewish People in the First Century.* 2 volumes. Philadelphia, PA: Fortress Press, 1976.

Sandmel, Samuel. *A Jewish Understanding of the New Testament.* Ho-boken, NJ: KTAV Publishing House, Inc. 1974.

Sandmel, Samuel. *Antisemitism in the New Testament?* Philadelphia, PA. Fortress Press, 1978.

Sandmel, Samuel. *The First Christian Century Judaism and Christian-ity: Certainties and Uncertainties.* New York, NY: Oxford University Press, 1969. (Lecture 2).

Strack, Herman L. *Introduction to the Talmud and Midrash.* Philadel-phia, PA: The Jewish Publication Society, 1939. (Part 1, Chapter 1; Part 2, Chapters 15–23).

Talmage, F. E. ed. *Disputation and Dialogue: Readings in the Jewish-Christian Encounter.* Hoboken, NJ: KTAV Publishing House, Inc., 1975.

Urbach, Ephraim E. *The Sages, Their Concepts and Beliefs.* Jerusalem: The Hebrew University Press, 1975. (Volume I, Chapters 2 and 4).

Index of Gospel Texts

Index of Rabbinic Texts